Lean Daily Management for Healthcare Field Book

Lean Daily Management for Healthcare Field Book

Gerard A. Berlanga · Brock C. Husby

CRC Press
Taylor & Francis Group
Boca Raton   London   New York

CRC Press is an imprint of the
Taylor & Francis Group, an **informa** business

A PRODUCTIVITY PRESS BOOK

CRC Press
Taylor & Francis Group
6000 Broken Sound Parkway NW, Suite 300
Boca Raton, FL 33487-2742

© 2017 by Taylor & Francis Group, LLC
CRC Press is an imprint of Taylor & Francis Group, an Informa business

No claim to original U.S. Government works

Printed on acid-free paper
Version Date: 20160531

International Standard Book Number-13: 978-1-4987-5650-1 (Paperback)

Library of Congress Cataloging-in-Publication Data

Names: Berlanga, Gerard A., author. | Husby, Brock C., author.
Title: Lean daily management for healthcare field book / Gerard A. Berlanga
and Brock C. Husby.
Description: Boca Raton : Taylor & Francis, 2016. | Includes index.
Identifiers: LCCN 2016003773 | ISBN 9781498756501 (alk. paper)
Subjects: | MESH: Health Facility Administration--methods | Health Services
Administration | Leadership | Organizational Culture | Quality Improvement
Classification: LCC RA971 | NLM WX 150.1 | DDC 362.1068--dc23
LC record available at http://lccn.loc.gov/2016003773

Visit the Taylor & Francis Web site at
http://www.taylorandfrancis.com

and the CRC Press Web site at
http://www.crcpress.com

Printed and bound in the United States of America by Publishers Graphics,
LLC on sustainably sourced paper.

Dedication

To my loving wife, Bonnie, who gave me the inspiration
to write this book and my late mother, Pauline,
who dedicated her life to our family.

Jerry Berlanga

To the wonderful and dedicated leaders, staff, and physicians
at Guadalupe Regional Medical Center, who on a daily basis
reminded me why I love doing the work that I do through their
passion and focus on serving patients and the community.

Brock Husby, PhD

Contents

Foreword

The success of a new Lean initiative for an organization largely depends on whether there are sustainment efforts and mechanisms in place to support the continuity of such an initiative or not. The transformation of the healthcare industry to be a more patient-centered service enterprise has been a noble goal which requires more than just the promise of contemporary system improvement methods such as Lean and Six Sigma techniques. Piecemeal redesign of healthcare elements with a catalog of successful improvement projects will be beneficial to patients; however, the sustainment of improvements remains the key to any healthcare organization seeking better quality and overall patient experience. Most of the gains from Lean initiatives eventually run into challenges with either sustaining the gains, spreading Lean gains to the rest of the organization, or losing senior leadership's support. The key to a lasting Lean healthcare transformation is to establish a management system for leaders to follow on a day-to-day basis.

A Lean daily management (LDM) system is a disciplined daily approach for an organization to develop its staff, align their efforts, and build a holistic and meaningful set of activities that will help achieve an organization's goals. It fosters a culture of continuous process improvement at the level of greatest value and empowers those doing the work to implement data driven improvements that they believe patients value most. It also enables teams and leaders to communicate daily about root cause challenges and visualizes progress on improvement initiatives. Jerry and Brock have extensive background and experience in applications of Lean concepts and tools in healthcare. They have served as Associate Vice Presidents, coaches, and strategists for lean transformation and operations excellence of leadership teams for several healthcare organizations across the United States and Canada. Their insight into linking LDM to sustainable continuous improvement transformation is a must for healthcare leaders to develop the new habits required to sustain Lean improvements. This book gives readers the important know-how for deploying LDM in their organizations.

F. Frank Chen, PhD
Luther Brown Distinguished Chair
Center for Advanced Manufacturing & Lean Systems
The University of Texas at San Antonio

Preface

This field book is a result of years of practicing, teaching, and coaching Lean principles and methods to healthcare leaders and front-line staff across the United States and Canada, as well as many hard-earned lessons and much trial-and-error experimentation to figure out how to make these principles work in a healthcare (and service) environment. Traditional Lean healthcare implementations delivered great short term results, but frequently lost steam as key Lean leaders moved on to other departments or organizations or they solely focused on large projects (such as VSM) or tools (such as 5S). This often led to obscuring the vision of organizations from the true potential of what transformational change their organization was capable of. Lean felt very much like a "push" onto the organization in the form of rapid improvement "Kaizen" projects or large-scale "Value Stream Mapping" projects and associated training that pulled in only a small percentage of leaders and staff and occurred infrequently. When Lean was introduced into organizations in this fashion (as a small number of very discrete "events" or "tools"), this definition of what lean "is" often became crystalized into the mind and culture of the organization, and handicapped the organization from making further progress. The initiatives often devolved into "Popcorn Kaizen" where lots of activity was taking place, but it didn't link together, change culture, or result in fundamental or long-lasting change.

In healthcare, the underlying waste isn't "overproduction" as we were taught in traditional manufacturing style Lean training. The underlying waste in healthcare is "underutilizing the creativity of our employees/staff" and the broken (or missing) management systems that most healthcare organizations struggle to operate within. This waste, and the accompanying opportunity, is even greater in healthcare than in other industries because staffing costs are a significantly higher proportion of expenses in healthcare than in manufacturing. Therefore, the vast experience, passion, knowledge, education, and commitment of the staff are an amazing and positive untapped opportunity.

How do we create a "pull" for Lean in healthcare? How do we utilize the creativity of our employees and providers across the entire organization in a way that is sustainable over the long term? How do we truly create a Lean transformation that engages all staff and leaders more effectively and meaningfully? These questions drove Brock and myself to look much more closely at Toyota style management principles and methods. Lean daily management (LDM) was indeed the "missing piece" in the Toyota house (or at least missing to Brock and me). At Toyota, LDM is integral to their effectiveness, but, like most true aspects of culture, we take it for granted and are hardly even aware it is there. It is similar to the structural framework of a house—you don't see it or are not consciously aware that it is there until there is a problem with it! In most healthcare organizations, there has never been an effective management system in place, so most healthcare organizations and leaders didn't "feel" this missing piece. Once leaders truly embrace this and see the power of it, they find it difficult to imagine managing without it! This is the reason that we are discussing the mechanics very clearly and practically in this book, to help practitioners and leaders figure out the critical but challenging task of building a robust and meaningful LDM system to help their organizations and improvement efforts.

This field book is intended to be used on the floor by healthcare leaders, providers, and staff to support LDM and Lean implementation. Healthcare leaders, providers, and staff continue to take on greater levels of complexity in their workplace, yet do not have effective management systems that engage leaders and staff in problem solving and improvement daily.

Many leading healthcare organizations across the United States and Canada are realizing that LDM is the first step (not the last step!) in their Lean transformation, but don't know where to start or which pitfalls to avoid. This field book gives them a step-by-step guide to LDM implementation and successful Lean transformation.

Guadalupe Regional Medical Center (GRMC) is our model LDM site for this field book, and has been a wonderful partner to work with. Working with this great organization is a constant reminder of why we love to do the work that we do with healthcare organizations! Their entire leadership team embraced the philosophy of "lead from the front" and has supported and allowed LDM and Lean to grow strongly within their organization. Their senior team was the first to be taught the principles of LDM, and wanted to thoroughly understand and believe in the power of these approaches before spreading it more broadly, which is a sign of their true leadership. They had the perfect balance of "healthy skepticism," optimism, and trust to grow process improvement and LDM in their organization in a positive way. GRMC has more successes and wins with every passing day. Also, as the LDM and Lean system has spread at GRMC, a number of "natural problem solvers" have emerged that surprise me daily with their intuitive understanding and eagerness to learn the principles. It is truly "in their DNA" to do LDM and process improvement, which is another daily inspiration for us as facilitators. GRMC leaders and staff have created a daily cadence for improvement which "pulls" ideas from staff and leaders based on daily LDM board performance.

This field book would not have been possible without the contribution of the following people: Joaquin Martinez, Travis Haynes (GRMC), Michelle Rumbaut (GRMC), Robert Haynes (GRMC), Daphne Blake, RN (GRMC), Fay Bennett (GRMC), Lauren Carter (GRMC), Penny Wallace (GRMC), Sheri Williams, RN (GRMC), Jennifer Valadez (GRMC), Brad White, Steven White, MD. (GRMC), Elizabeth Pastrano (GRMC), Richard Power (GRMC/Morrison), Dennis Wingler (GRMC/Morrison), Steve Peth (GRMC), Amanda Davila (GRMC), Brook Brown (GRMC), Douglas Leslie (GRMC), Karen Oncken (GRMC), Dolores Major, MD (GRMC), GRMC Board of Directors, D.J. "Dave" Calkins, Board Chair (GRMC), Jacquelin Talley (GRMC), Veronica San Miguel (GRMC), Dr. Frank Chen (UTSA), Dr. Wan (UTSA), Bonnie Berlanga, Oscar Avena, Kristine Mednansky (CRC Press), as well as a multitude of others who helped us learn these principles and methods over the years!

Authors

Jerry Berlanga has over 20 years of Lean Six Sigma experience and has lead and supported Lean Six Sigma transformations with key organizations such as CPS Energy, USAA, Baylor Scott & White Healthcare, and other leading organizations across the United States and Canada.

Jerry is a respected Lean Six Sigma teacher, coach, and author. He currently co-teaches a 1-day University of Texas at San Antonio (UTSA) Lean Daily Management workshop. Jerry founded UTSA's continuous improvement professionals (CIP) group several years ago to bring Lean Six Sigma professionals together to share innovations, best practices, and advances in Lean Six Sigma and create mentorships, internships, and job opportunities for junior Lean coaches and engineers. Jerry invites readers to contact him at jerry@leanproviders.com to learn more about Lean daily management.

Brock Husby, PhD, is a Lean consultant, speaker, and researcher and was an associate vice president (AVP) at Baylor Scott & White Health, where he was an integral part of the deployment of a holistic Lean approach, including system-wide training, projects (A3, VSM, Lean Layout, and Kaizen), Hoshin planning, foundational and advanced tools, and an extensive deployment and maturation of Lean management systems. Brock was also a process assurance and corrective actions engineer for the Space Shuttle Program at the Kennedy Space Center and a technical assistant at *Car and Driver* magazine. Brock earned BSE, MSE, and PhD degrees in Industrial & Operations Engineering from the University of Michigan, Ann Arbor. Brock was one of the first three AHRQ grant-funded industrial engineers at Denver Health and Hospital System who trained and mentored their initial class of "Lean black-belts," helped create the foundational structure for their Lean program, and facilitated the initial rapid improvement (RIE/Kaizen) events. The results of these initial efforts demonstrated operational expense savings of $124,000,000 (as of 2013), as well as Denver Health becoming the first healthcare delivery organization to win the Shingo Prize for operational excellence (2011).

Chapter 1

What's Been Missing with Lean Healthcare Transformations?

Brock, myself, and most of the Lean professionals we worked closely with over the years learned Lean from reading leading Lean books, practicing Lean in our organizations, apprenticing under established Lean senseis and reflecting on what worked, what didn't work, and what we could do differently (our own practitioner plan–do–study–act [PDSA] cycle so to speak).

We learned Lean as a system (pulling from the Toyota production system "House" model, see Figure 1.1). We trained and coached leaders, managers, and front-line staff on the key Lean principles from the Toyota house and then launched key Lean initiatives. This usually started with identifying strategic value streams, key A3s or Kaizen events or rapid improvement projects to not only achieve key organizational goals but to also develop staff along the way. Leaders and teams quickly learned the power of Lean methods and life was good.

At some point in our Lean practice, Brock and I started to realize that most of the Lean gains we had worked so hard to put in place with leaders and staff eventually would run into challenges with sustaining their gains or spreading Lean gains to the rest of the organization or losing senior leadership's support.

We started to think that maybe there was something we had been missing in our Lean healthcare transformations, but what was it?

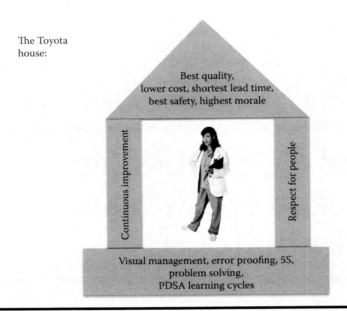

Figure 1.1   The Toyota house.

We knew that senior leadership was the key to a lasting Lean healthcare transformation, but we hadn't really changed or improved the management processes and model that our leaders followed on a day-to-day basis.

We launched value stream maps (VSMs) in the operating room (OR), emergency department (ED), and key service lines across the hospital and clinics dramatically improving quality, lead times, revenue, patient satisfaction, and eliminating waste along the way. Over time we found ourselves re-launching VSMs year after year to keep the improvement momentum going, along the way we were getting feedback from staff that leadership wasn't really engaging as much as staff needed them to.

Lean daily management (LDM) tip: A common mistake is to focus on the application of individual tools first. This can lead to some great "point improvements" (also known as "popcorn Kaizen") but doesn't lead to overall system improvements. It is equivalent to teaching a person how to use a wrench, screwdriver, welding torch, and other tools and asking the person to assemble a car from a pile of parts. The knowledge of the use of individual tools doesn't aggregate into the relational knowledge or integrating knowledge that is critical for building an effective system (which a car is an aggregation of countless parts that, when working properly, results in a smooth running, safe, and reliable vehicle). This is why many hospitals quantify impacts on individual projects that are very impressive, but the aggregate impact on the overall organization usually doesn't reflect this level of impact "on the books." Another way to describe it is suboptimization, where individual processes or issues are addressed in a one-by-one fashion and not linked together resulting in a very suboptimal system full of seemingly "optimized" parts. The significance of addressing this breakdown is critical in all organizations, but particularly so in healthcare. In the manufacturing industry, the customer who receives the end product is affected by the price, quality, function, and other aspects of the product. In healthcare, the customer is actually "inside the factory walls" and their experience is directly affected by both the reality and perception of the processes and flow within. Therefore, a suboptimized and fragmented system easily leads to many of the negative perceptions (and realities!) of patients who receive care in the U.S. healthcare system—extremely expensive, disorganized, not patient-focused, full of delays and inefficiency, and often resulting in poor patient-care and outcomes.

Beginning our Lean journey is the same approach to building a house. We need a good foundation, no matter how good the construction of the house is. Without a solid foundation, it will start to fall apart and won't last long. But this begs the question, why is the foundation so commonly skipped? Just like with a house, the foundation is taken for granted until something goes wrong! It isn't glamorous and is often not thought about when it is working, but when something goes wrong, it is clear that everything that is built on top of it is threatened by a compromised foundation. When Lean practitioners skip the "foundation" and begin working with advanced tools and techniques (such as VSM to tackle inpatient length-of-stay [LOS]) without having developed their leaders and staff, without standard work and visual management, and other foundational tools, they really struggle to implement their new process and even if they succeed temporarily, it doesn't sustain! This is equivalent to building your house on a foundation of sand with a natural spring below it!

Toyota's "House" model is what we followed and implemented within our organizations; however, something seemed to be missing. Over time we realized that Toyota's "House" model assumes that you have an *effective LDM system*. In the foundation, Toyota identifies visual management, 5S, error proofing, PDSA learning cycles, A3 problem solving and other foundational principles and tools, but doesn't really explain or define the "management system" that must be in place to ensure leaders and staff are following through. One might wonder why Toyota left this out of their model. One explanation for this is that one of the best ways to define culture is "the way we do things around here." Over the many decades that Toyota developed the Toyota production system (TPS), the development of an effective management system, with active problem solving at all levels, engaged visible leaders and a focus on data and effective goal setting were all at the core of the TPS and a critical part of its culture ("the way we do things around here"). Therefore, it was such an embedded part of its culture that it didn't get explicitly placed on the Toyota house (see Figure 1.1). Unfortunately, in most U.S. organizations, and especially in healthcare, those aspects of a management system are chronically deficient, and this lack of explicit integration and facilitation within organizations has led to the chronic and perplexing struggles that organizations have had in deploying and sustaining Lean.

Error proofing, 5S, A3 problem solving, PDSA learning cycles, and visual management are all foundational Lean principles, but when implemented without a LDM system, they take much longer to implement, feel like a "push" from management and are much less likely to be sustained over the long haul. This can also result in the concept of suboptimization mentioned earlier, where the foundational tools are applied "in a vacuum" and not used to build a system, so the critical foundational Lean concepts and tools are either applied haphazardly, incorrectly, or not at all. Given that these are foundational Lean tools and most organizations only give them cursory consideration before moving on to the "advanced tools" of Lean, their struggles with culture change and sustainment are not unexpected.

As mentioned earlier, LDM is fundamentally "assumed" to exist, but doesn't in most organizations. The normal "trajectory" for most healthcare systems in the United States that have been early adopters of applying Lean principles have been to start with Lean projects (such as VSMs or Kaizen/rapid improvement events), tackle larger and more complex projects, do some peripheral A3s (smaller focused projects), and then experiment with LDM once they are much further along on their Lean journey. In essence, they are treating LDM as an "advanced tool," and adding it on further down their journey. The perspective that the authors are proposing is that LDM is an "over-arching foundational tool" or a subfoundational tool that should be applied first.

LDM tip: Develop and help leaders learn Lean as a management system first, then focus on key Lean foundational tools and methods such as 5S, standard work, etc. (see Figure 1.2).

LDM addresses the gaps in management processes, which often are never truly addressed in a Lean deployment/transformation. Most successful Lean transformations we have been a part of have had strong leaders that made Lean a priority and tried very hard to engrain Lean thinking into their leadership team, but as soon as that leader or Lean champion left the organization, the organization eventually slid back. In essence, the charismatic senior leader sustained the change through "force of will," persistence, and basic good management practices. While the leader was in place and saying, "this was a priority" for them, enough leaders and staff within the organization followed suit, even if they didn't fully understand or believe in the approach (i.e., they knew that to be successful in the organization they needed to "play along"). Without a formal LDM training program, daily practice, and coaching, healthcare leaders will not develop the new habits required to sustain Lean improvements.

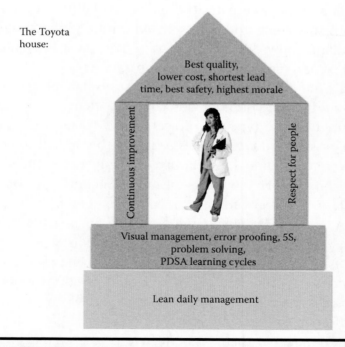

The Toyota house:

Figure 1.2   Modified Toyota house model with Lean daily management (LDM) "subfoundation."

Another aspect of LDM that is significant for organizations wanting to truly drive organizational and cultural change lies in the neuroscience of habit formation. When an individual is following a "tried and true" process, they are aware of the beginning and end of the associated activities, but the rest is essentially "on autopilot" (essentially, it is hardwired in the brain). When a new process or way of thinking is being undertaken, it is very difficult and challenging, as every step needs to be thought of consciously, and it is very easy to slip back to the "old habits" (i.e., the path of least resistance). To transform a new task, way of thinking, or job into a new habit requires numerous iterations and a dedication to this undertaking, which then eventually results in a new habit being formed. In most organizations, and especially in healthcare, most of the "habits" are learned through one of three primary (but overlapping and related) paths: (1) we have always done it this way, (2) I learned this approach at my previous organization or where I was trained, and (3) being "thrown to the wolves" to learn my new job from "tribal knowledge" haphazardly gained through shadowing the work practices, work-arounds, short-cuts, and good or bad habits of my coworkers.

To take a more deliberate path to establishing habits, and creating a culture of problem solving and habits based on the foundational Lean tools, requires a fundamentally different approach than most Lean healthcare organizations take. When most healthcare organizations start with large VSM or Kaizen projects, these are very large "boluses" of change that require extensive resources and a huge number of "habits" to change at once.

Not surprisingly, these types of projects rarely sustain or survive to full deployment. First of all, the resources required to conduct them limit their frequency, and any individual or team would only experience a Lean VSM or Kaizen project once every few years (at most). Second, the "bolus" of change means that a large number of habits need to change all at once, and there is no mechanism or "project management" framework to truly help it be implemented or integrated/experimented with until it really works.

Most "process owners" in hospitals are highly successful clinical or operational staff who were promoted into managerial positions (due to their technical or professional proficiency and/or expertise), which requires a completely different skill set and approach compared with their previous role. For the rare manager that is an effective project manager and change management expert, the results come very naturally. For the remainder, the results generally don't materialize. They realize that they are "in over their heads" and really struggle to be effective, and many figure out how to "survive" by mimicking the habits and approaches of their peers. This usually takes the form of "avoiding getting in trouble" and learning what management really focuses on and cares about, which is (in most cases) avoiding major incidences with patients, maintaining their budget, and avoiding negative HR issues. With large Lean events (such as VSMs), the amount of technical and process change, and the number of habits and behaviors that need to change are simply too much, and a condition of "cognitive overload" overwhelms the team and leaders, and they revert to just "doing the work" rather than also "improving the work." Without an effective management system, the sponsors (who have senior level ownership and responsibility) and other senior leaders involved in the project don't follow up effectively or consistently, and the Lean project "dies on the vine" without ever realizing the potential that it initially promised, which is all-too-common of a situation for any Lean practitioner!

With LDM, the issue of habit formation is hardwired into the approach of looking at LDM as a subfoundational tool/approach. By hardwiring in a daily discipline of LDM board review, applying foundational tools, and following the "scientific method" in their daily work, Lean-conducive habits begin to be formed, comfort with foundational Lean tools increase, and basic skills of project management (i.e., implementing action items) are established. Leaders and staff truly begin to wear two hats while at work, "do the work" and "improve the work" (see Figure 1.3), which fundamentally differentiates

1. Do the work <u>and</u>...

2. Improve the work!

Figure 1.3 LDM concept of wearing two hats: (1) "do the work" and (2) "improve the work."

Toyota from all of their competitors. Toyota's management system ensures these two hats are practiced by staff and leaders.

> *Why not make the work easier and more interesting so that people do not have to sweat? The Toyota style is not to create results by working hard. It is a system that says there is no limit to the people's creativity. People don't go to Toyota to 'work', they go there to 'think'.*
>
> **–Taiichi Ohno**

Respect for People

Healthcare organizations arguably rely more on their highly trained and highly skilled staff (people) more than any other industry (due to a relative lack of automation and a disproportionate share of expenses being staff and salary), thus "Respect for People" takes on more meaning when we start our Lean transformation in healthcare. Special care must be taken to ensure clinical and nonclinical staff engage in Lean in ways that align with patient care, safety, and quality, along with our more traditional productivity and throughput measures. Our people are the greatest resource we have, and the fundamental waste we have is *not utilizing their experience and creativity to solve problems*. We oftentimes jump to key organizational goals and challenges; however, Lean in healthcare means starting with goals and challenges that engage staff in problems they face on the floor every day, then gradually moving to key organizational goals. With this approach, we are taking the time to focus on developing our people first, and ironically this is the fastest path to achieving key organizational goals!

Celebration!

In the high stakes, high-stress healthcare environment, it is easy to always focus on the gaps. You MUST help your teams celebrate, even small wins, or even worthwhile failures! This is critical to the long-term cultural transformation. Work with your communications, human resources, or marketing department to communicate wins within the organization, and help your teams celebrate and get recognition. This can be done through a hospital performance evaluation/incentive system, manager's meetings, hospital newsletters, thank-you notes from leaders, promotion, development, or any multitude of means. More fundamentally, it can be done right at your LDM board or in the department, with a simple thank-you and recognition of the team's efforts and success! This provides positive reinforcement, and evidence has shown that recognition and a perception of meaning and significance to one's work is a more powerful motivator for staff than is a financial reward and this just takes a little time, sincerity, and follow-through on the part of leaders!

> *Success is not final, failure is not fatal: it is the courage to continue that counts.*
>
> **–Sir Winston Churchill**

Exercise: As you prepare for your Lean transformation think about what "Respect for People" means in your organization:
Take a quick assessment of your organization's "Respect for People"

1. Do leaders provide clearly aligned organizational goals for staff that can be tracked and managed daily or weekly?
2. Is staff aware of their progress toward these goals on a daily or weekly basis?
3. Are leaders pulling in ideas from staff on these key goals daily/weekly?
4. Are leaders coaching/developing staff problem solving on these key goals daily/weekly?
5. Is staff engaged in measuring, tracking, and improving their key goals on a daily/weekly basis?
6. Are leaders following up with staff to ensure they are making progress daily/weekly?
7. Are leaders "pulling up" ideas that staff may be stuck on or who need higher-level attention or focus?
8. Are leaders recognizing and celebrating small and big wins (as well as failures that have taught us things)?

> *"Having no problem is the biggest problem of all."*
>
> **–Taiichi Ohno**

"No problem" is the problem, and the journey is more important than the goal. The focus of Lean is always on developing your people as better problem solvers and solving meaningful problems! Without problems, there would be no learning, without which there is no development of your staff. Therefore, identification of problems and coaching of your staff along the problem-solving journey result in the development of your staff!

Increased complexity, regulatory demands, and an ever-changing marketplace require organizations to improve to simply maintain existing levels of performance. What was "good" yesterday may not "cut it" tomorrow. The more staff we can engage in improvement, the greater chance we have to not only maintain existing levels of performance, but exceed them. The key is encouraging experimentation and oftentimes failure! Experimentation creates a learning process, where what you expect to happen versus what actually happens is critical to learning. In between the two is learning, and failure is an option! (vs. not an option in non-Lean organizations).

Lean Projects versus LDM ("Pulling" Lean vs. "Pushing" Lean)

Organizations often copy the more obvious parts of Lean (i.e., 5S, Kaizen, A3 problem solving, etc.). The problem with a tool-based approach is that Lean doesn't grow, mature, and really get into the "DNA" of their organization. *Lean is perceived by leaders and staff as a "project based" improvement method instead of an everyday problem-solving culture.*

An example of this is the historic focus early on with identifying and implementing key value streams within a hospital. Starting with two or three key value streams inevitably takes a large cross-functional team from various departments within the organization. Team members are often pulled from various departments to support a Lean value stream design and implementation. These team members are identified by an executive sponsor and are pulled together to focus on one key value stream and it's key goals. A Lean coach supports both the executive sponsor and the team through design and implementation of this very lengthy process (8 months to 1 year to fully implement). There is usually great energy and excitement early on and the team quickly identifies key wastes/gaps in the value stream. A future state value stream is designed to address the wastes and gaps (as well as the value stream goals) and the team starts implementing their action plan. Thirty days in, the team starts to see quick wins, 60 days in, the team realizes even greater wins, 90 days in, the team celebrates achieving some major milestones, then something interesting happens—staff start to lose steam/leadership seems to lose or shift focus. New "fires" occur, leaders get pulled into other key initiatives and projects, and staff is left to implement the rest of their action plan with declining leadership support and real functional pressures to spend more time in their respective departments versus a cross functional team. The Lean coach must now re-engage the team and leader after 8 months or 1 year and "re-cast" another value stream effort to regain the momentum that was lost. What happened here?

The missing piece is culture and developing our people, which takes a long-term perspective and focus. A subset of this is our management culture. It doesn't just "happen" on its own without a deliberate investment of time, energy, and focus of the organization to make it a priority. *Organizations usually expect their staff to do continuous improvement, but the management system and culture actually "punish" staff for doing the right things. This punishment can come from making long-term problems "visible" (which an ineffective management system sees as creating a problem, or making a department "look bad"), through slightly decreased productivity due to the investment of time to do problem solving, and departments that focus on true problem solving rather than simply "gaming the system" so that their performance looks good according to the (potentially) corrupt organizational performance management and evaluation system.*

> *Lean Daily Management creates a culture of accountability, problem solving at all levels of the organization at a daily cadence.... It changes "the way we do things around here" (i.e., "our culture") from just "doing the work" (one hat) to also "improving the work" (the second hat). It makes problem identification something to celebrate, develops our people and leaders, and adds more meaning and alignment to our organization's daily tasks. LDM essentially creates a variety of different productive and meaningful new "habits" that will differentiate our hospital and help support its future growth and success!*

LDM requires leaders to change the inherently broken management processes first. Leaders first learn LDM by attending an LDM workshop or training event. Leaders then build the four components of the LDM system: (1) LDM boards, (2) leader rounds, (3) leader daily discipline, and (4) lean project management.

As leadership practices LDM, middle management, and front-line staff practice as well, and LDM is set in motion. Key front-line staff LDM boards are stood up with senior leaders and middle managers that have been practicing LDM already. Leaders learn how to round effectively, LDM problem-solve effectively and leader's daily discipline ensures follow through.

The cadence for improvement happens daily/weekly versus monthly or quarterly and staff start to problem-solve around their key unit goals; ideas/

actions that staff are struggling with escalate daily/weekly. This greater frequency helps to establish the critical and meaningful habits that we discussed previously that are essential to developing LDM and growing Lean within the organization.

Before LDM, Lean efforts were predominantly a "Push" from leadership to the frontlines, with executive sponsors or other senior leaders as the primary force to keep them moving forward. Now, with a maturing LDM system, front-line staff are problem solving within their natural functional teams on problems within their power to affect. As bigger problems come up, front-line teams start "pulling" for Lean methods and tools such as Kaizens, value stream mapping, A3 problem solving, 5S, and other Lean tools/methods. Lean becomes the "way" they address their complex problems/challenges and LDM becomes the foundation for support and follow through.

With LDM in place, Lean can now spread much faster than before. LDM boards and leader rounds allow ideas to spread across the organization much faster than before simply because more of the leadership team and staff are engaged than just a few dedicated cross-functional team members on a VSM project or several Kaizen events.

With LDM in place, leaders can focus the organization like never before on key goals such as reducing "no shows" or improving "patient satisfaction" and move the dial much faster because, again, more leaders and more staff are engaged.

LDM is key to any Lean transformation because it first exposes staff to the business in a way that they haven't seen before. They have clarity on what key LDM board goals they are tracking and managing daily. The "habit" of daily problem solving is established and reinforced, and leaders are engaged and provide context to the work that the teams are doing. Once staff is exposed to their LDM board goals and the rounding process, they begin to engage in tracking, analyzing, and developing ideas to achieve their LDM board goals with the coaching and support of their leaders and the rounding process. As staff and leaders engage on a daily basis with their LDM board's goals they begin to "pull" support from leadership, which empowers them and gives them the confidence to continually improve. Engaged leaders and staff will soon find that they can only achieve so much in a departmental/ functional way and they soon start integrating their LDM boards and rounding with other functional areas both upstream and downstream or even those supporting units such as housekeeping and information technology. Integration gets the organization thinking and problem solving in a service line– or process-centered way or across departmental lines, which opens up bigger opportunities for improvement and innovation. Alignment of strategy to our LDM system and all LDM boards, leader rounds and leader daily disciplines not only points everyone to the organization's true north and drives them closer to that strategy daily, but it also helps prevent redundant, wasteful efforts that could take valuable resources away from supporting the daily problems that escalate from our leader rounds (Figure 1.4).

One Size Fits All?

There are small, medium, large, and extra-large problems within our organization, so a "one size fits all approach" won't work. When organizations use a traditional approach to deploying Lean, they often start with VSMs, Kaizen, or rapid improvement events (RIEs), 5S, or other similar approaches deployed organization-wide. As Lean is introduced to an organization, this often defines "Lean" for most of the organization, as it is (to a large extent) crystallized in their mind as discrete improvement projects that come from management. With LDM, staff sees Lean as small teams identifying and solving problems on a continuous basis, and are empowered to problem solving, escalate problems, and "own" their problems. This is a much more desirable way to start and crystallize their understanding of Lean rather than it being a large, time intensive, and exhausting 3–5 days event that happens once every couple of years with results that don't sustain effectively.

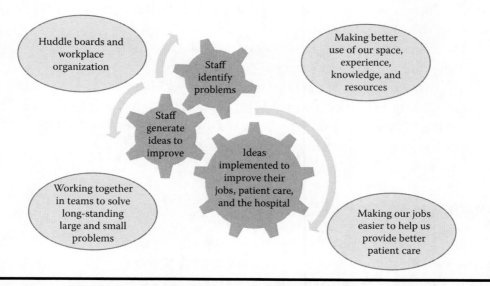

Figure 1.4 Virtuous cycle of continuous improvement using LDM.

There Is No "Silver Bullet"

Instead of talking about Lean tools, it is better to see this effort as part of the management system, integrating practices that will bring results.

> *...the ultimate arrogance is to change the way people work without changing the way we manage them.*
>
> **–John Toussaint, MD and Roger Gerard, PhD**

Things to Remember

1. *Failure is an option*—If our staff fear failure more than the potential benefit of trying out a new idea, we have lost the battle and the war.
2. *Respect for people*—Violating this principle has huge consequences, and moves through the organization like wildfire. Our people are the greatest resources we have, and the fundamental waste we have is to not utilize their experience and creativity to solve problems.
3. *No problem is a BIG PROBLEM*—Encouraging experimentation and failure, the journey is more important than the goal.
4. *Experiment*—Use the scientific method and learn from our failures.
5. *Lead by example*—As a leader, see for yourself how the work is being done. Go to the Gemba, where the work is done.
6. *Celebrate!*—You must help your teams celebrate, even small wins, or even worthwhile failures.
7. *Focus on establishing new habits!*—Habits are the key to success, at the individual, team, and leadership level.
8. *There is no "silver bullet" or "one size fits all" approach*—Focus on developing your people and LDM boards first, and the "pull" will come for the bigger and more high-impact projects when the time is right and your teams have reached the right level.

Journal

This is your opportunity to process and creatively express your ideas. You can write *questions* you still have, *responses* that were significant to you, or simply *summarize* your thoughts.

Be creative!

Chapter 2

What Is Lean Daily Management?

Lean Daily Management System

The Lean daily management (LDM) system is defined as, "A disciplined system for developing our staff, aligning our efforts, and building a holistic and meaningful improvement system that will help achieve our organization's goal." It is divided into four parts (see Figure 2.1).

A critical aspect of developing this new management system is to have a mechanism for problems to "rise to the right level." Leaders coach, develop, and encourage their staff to problem-solve at the front-line unit level first. Problems that the front-line units struggle with are escalated to the middle management level primarily through daily middle management leader rounds. Problems that cannot get addressed at the middle management level escalate to the senior leadership level through daily/weekly senior leadership rounds. We often have problems "festering" at a lower level with no awareness at the higher levels where the knowledge, resources, and expertise are to address these issues. This escalation can just be a corner of your staff's LDM board but requires leaders to round regularly and take these issues as "homework" and follow up with their teams.

Ironically, one of the primary reasons that escalation doesn't happen naturally is that problems generally aren't solved at their correct level.

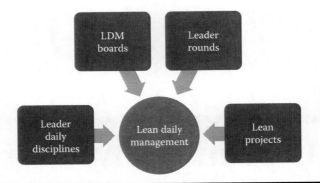

Figure 2.1   Four part Lean daily management model.

Problems that could be solved at the frontline or at a lower level get escalated one or two levels too high, and end up "bottlenecking" our leaders so they don't have time to focus on problems that require their level of expertise, knowledge, and/or experience. Therefore, our senior leaders and best resources for driving, supporting, and developing our organization are inundated with dealing with "minutia" and they don't have the time or focus to "grow the business" or do anything other than firefighting. If you don't believe this, just go and ask some of your middle management and supervisors what percentage of their time is spent with dealing with putting out "fires," dealing with seemingly petty problems, and other similar issues. By pushing problem solving to "its lowest level" (those closest to the problem have the greatest knowledge of the processes, as well as visibility of the issues to successfully solve and implement and own the solutions), we free up the time and capability of our leaders and managers, allow them time to solve problems that are escalated, and work on "growing the business" (see Figure 2.2).

> *A leader is best when people barely know he exists, when his work is done, his aim fulfilled, they will say: we did it ourselves.*
>
> **–Lao Tzu**

> *Leadership is solving problems. The day soldiers stop bringing you their problems is the day you have stopped leading them. They have either lost confidence that you can help or concluded you do not care. Either case is a failure of leadership.*
>
> **–Colin Powell**

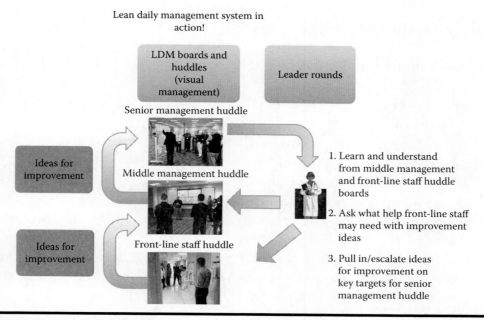

Figure 2.2 Escalation process.

It is better to lead from behind and to put others in front, especially when you celebrate victory when nice things occur. You take the front line when there is danger. Then people will appreciate your leadership.

–Nelson Mandela

Leader daily discipline establishes the leaders' plan and "cadence" for executing their LDM system (what LDM boards to review/round with, what days to round with key units/LDM boards, etc.) with staff, peers, and boss with respect to key daily, weekly, and monthly leadership tasks.

Leader daily discipline is key because it sets expectations with staff, peers, and the boss when key tasks will be performed and starts to take leaders from more of a firefighting "crisis" management mode to more of a consistent cadence.

Leader daily discipline enables consistent development of new managers coming into our organization by clearly outlining key leadership tasks or activities that occur daily, weekly, and monthly. New leaders quickly learn "how things get done" within the organization.

Question: How could we take aspects of this and hardwire into our leaders daily discipline?

Leader Daily Discipline Exercise

Let's take 5 minutes to list a typical day:

1. Write down a typical (yesterday?) day from the moment you arrived to the moment you left.
2. Now, take a moment to review what worked really well and maybe what didn't work so well in that day.
3. What could you change or improve?
4. Take 5 minutes to now rewrite your new "best" day/daily routine (using the 80/20 rule, 20% of the time we will be overcome by unexpected events vs. the other way around).
5. Add in when you will conduct leader rounds and develop LDM boards with your staff (certain LDM boards on certain days), when you and your immediate staff will review LDM boards and when and how you will follow up on escalated ideas from your staff, etc.
6. Why are these daily habits so important to success?
7. Will we achieve our "best" daily routine right away?
8. What areas will we need to continually tweak to develop our "best" daily routine over time?
9. Why is having this routine so important to you and your staff?

Develop Your Cadence (Daily/Weekly/Monthly)

1. What is the cadence of your work and how can we develop meaning-ful leader daily discipline? (Is there any rhythm or cadence in your day/week/month? If so please write it out.)
2. What do we need to make sure we do on daily/weekly/monthly basis?
3. What issues or problems "creep up on us" and have us working through the weekend away from our family?
4. Make sure to include LDM boards, leadership rounds, updating our leadership daily discipline schedule!

Three Layers to Our LDM Board

There are three critical layers to our LDM board that will take some practice to perfect.

Top Layer (Symptoms)

The top layer is a run chart/visual graphic of a metric/goal/gap. This defines what we are trying to improve.

Middle Layer (Diagnosis)

The middle layer is the analysis. Why is there a gap between our daily goal and our performance today?

Bottom Layer (Treatment Plan)

The bottom layer is for action items/ideas. How will we close the gap?

LDM boards are generally well understood by staff and leaders and tend to go up relatively easily after they gain some familiarity and practice with the approach through effective training, coaching, and support; however, leadership rounds are a different story altogether (Figure 2.3). Even after LDM training, many leaders believe that they are already conducting "leadership rounds" in their own way/style and that they don't really need a coach or script to ensure they ask the key questions that ensure the LDM system is working. You will need to ensure that the three basic leadership

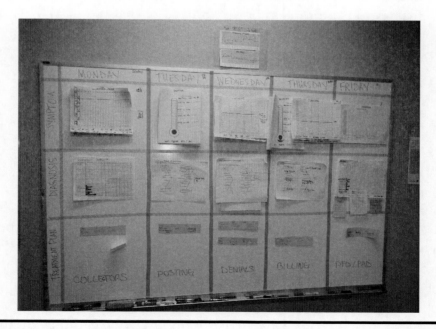

Figure 2.3   Working LDM board.

round conversations are addressed consistently by all leaders. Having a consistent leadership round script ensures that staff and leaders have the same consistent conversations and dialogue across the organization. Having scripting or a leader round checklist early on ensures that each section of the LDM board is being addressed (symptoms/progress toward goals are understood by staff; analysis/diagnosis of the problem has been thought through by staff and ideas/actions/treatment plans are in place and being implemented by staff to move their key LDM board goals in the right direction). Incomplete LDM boards (symptoms/goals not being tracked daily, empty diagnosis section–no analysis, and actions/ideas that haven't been implemented or updated) are a telltale sign of ineffective/inconsistent leadership rounds.

Leader round conversations:

Conversation 1: Staff explains progress on LDM board goals/symptoms. This ensures that staff understands and is very clear on the LDM board goals.

"Could you walk me through your LDM board and how it works on a daily basis?"

If different staff can't really explain how the LDM board works, or details of how the team is progressing, then it is a sign to the leader that there is a problem or disconnect, or that the LDM system needs to be further matured in this area.

Conversation 2: Staff explains the diagnosis, or "why," they might have missed goal (with respect to these goals/symptoms) and their treatment plans.

"What are you doing to improve the issues you identified on your LDM board?"

"Are you moving closer to your goal? If not, what is your team's plan?"

This ensures that staff is tracking progress toward their key goals/symptoms (the run chart portion of their LDM board). Staff should give specific answers that indicate how they did yesterday (actuals vs. goal) and they should be able to answer how much they were off (or met or beat!) their goal for the previous day as well as the last week in general (are we getting better over the last week or worse?). The more detail you get from staff on this question, the more you can ascertain how engaged they are in their LDM board goals and LDM process.

This conversation also ensures that staff is engaged in problem solving/analysis/diagnosis part of their LDM board and LDM system. Initially the leader may have to help get the problem solving started by asking key questions about "why" the gaps are there (using the Socratic method listed in the following). If staff can answer the "whys," make sure staff is asking "why" enough times (or using the fishbone diagram, which we will discuss in more detail later) to get to true root causes (be careful to not take over the problem solving for staff—simply ask them to think about deeper root causes/whys).

This conversation also ensures that staff are developing and implementing ideas/actions/treatment plan to address their key "whys" (root causes) as they relate to their LDM board's goals/symptoms. This is arguably the most important part of the LDM board and leadership round. Staff will often track LDM board's goals daily, but fail to complete the diagnosis/analysis section and then jump to treatment plan actions based on "anecdotal" assumptions that don't address the root causes (because they skipped the critical "diagnosis" section!). As you conduct leadership rounds, make sure all actions/ideas staff are implementing tie back to a diagnosis/root cause that in turn ties back to their LDM board's symptom/goal. These simple disconnects will happen as front-line staff struggle to understand the LDM system and their LDM board.

Conversation 3: Leader asks what help the staff needs with their LDM board:

> "Is there anything that I can do to help support your LDM board or your problem-solving efforts? Are there any issues that you need me to take up the chain of command to a higher level?"

This conversation ensures that first and foremost the symptoms, diagnosis, and treatment plan are well understood and that staff are getting support, whether it be more help with their LDM board to make sure the goals/symptoms they are tracking make sense, are clear and that the daily data they need to track performance is getting to them (initially the data may be pulled manually, over time the leader should be working to automate [when feasible] the data collection to make it easier for staff to track and manage their LDM board. Don't let the inability to pull data automatically stop you from measuring what really counts).

This third question also ensures that any ideas/actions from middle management and front-line unit LDM boards that staff are struggling with get escalated to the senior leadership LDM board for prioritization and resourcing (shown in Figure 2.4).

Figure 2.4 LDM board with escalated issue on it.

LDM Training

Setting up leadership LDM workshops to give leaders a condensed overview and an introduction to the key elements of LDM, as well as clearly outlining what new behaviors leaders will need to adopt will be key. Immediately after the LDM workshop, leaders must build their LDM boards (using their departmental goals and measures) and identify those key front-line units within their department to develop their first front-line unit LDM boards. Once the leader has established his or her own LDM board and the first key front-line unit LDM boards, leadership rounds need to be planned, scheduled (leader daily discipline plan), and conducted daily to reinforce LDM board tracking, management, learning, escalation of ideas and most importantly early on learning, coaching, and development of both staff and leader on the LDM system.

Schedule your leadership round "route" as part of our leader daily discipline plan by identifying which LDM boards you will "round" with on which days and at what times. Scheduling your rounds with staff creates a regular rhythm or "cadence" that they get familiar with and makes it easier for both leaders and staff to adopt the new LDM system. Many healthcare organizations cannot commit to a specific time each day to round initially, so leadership rounds can flex to the needs of leadership and staff; however, they do need to happen daily at the middle management level and at least weekly at the senior leadership level to ensure front-line unit LDM boards are kept up with and managed as well as to ensure ideas/problems that staff are stuck on get escalated and addressed.

Things to Remember

1. *LDM:* A disciplined system for developing our staff, aligning our efforts, and building a holistic and meaningful improvement system that will help achieve our organization's goals.
2. *Three key conversations staff presents to leadership for the leader round:*
   a. Staff reviews goals/symptoms.
   b. Staff reviews diagnosis or "why" they might have missed goal and their treatment plan.
   c. Leader asks what help may be needed with staff LDM boards and actions/ideas.
3. Leadership rounds are uniquely different than simply "management by walking around."
4. Go back and update your leader daily discipline.

Journal

This is your opportunity to process and creatively express your ideas. You can write *questions* you still have, *responses* that were significant to you, or simply *summarize* your thoughts.
   Be creative!

Chapter 3

Lean Daily Management Boards

One of the critical aspects of building a Lean daily management (LDM) system are the most tangible and obvious pieces of the system—the problem-solving boards that proliferate in a healthy and dynamic LDM! You might naturally ask what is different from these boards compared with the litany of white dry-erase or cork boards that litter most hospitals, as well as the "LDM problem-solving sessions" that occur around them in most hospitals, and the difference is very profound.

In most healthcare organizations, the term "huddles" are used ubiquitously, and this often represents a huge barrier to change. "Huddling" often elicits a response of "been there, done that," and this is one of the first hurdles to overcome. If you look at most of the boards that hang on the walls of most hospitals, they are full of policies, procedures, announcements, warnings, reminders, and other "static" information that rarely get looked at or updated. They are essentially "wallpaper" and serve no real purpose or function. They are meant for one-way information flow and conveyance of information, nothing more. When we do 5S (workplace organization) events in hospitals, we often find call-lists and other documents on the walls and boards of hospitals which are 20+ years old, often including invalid numbers, staff who no longer work there, and businesses that no longer exist. Other times, you remove a piece of paper from a wall or a board and the material underneath is a distinctly different color than around it, that is, the document, has been on the board or on the wall so long that the area around it has been bleached by the 20 years of fluorescent light! This reflects the fact that the staff haven't really looked at it in that long. This fact becomes obvious when a Lean method such as 5S forces them to look at these sort of items and they see the age of it; it is immediately taken down or updated.

If staff was looking at the document regularly, they would have already taken it down or updated it on their own. This is precisely the opposite of what an active LDM system board is intended to be a wallpaper! When something is static and unchanging in front of a staff member for a long time, it is actually "invisible" to them and meaningless.

The same applies to traditional huddles that are often one-way and the equivalent of static information being applied. This equivalency may be a little extreme, as there is still a need for operational and information sharing huddles, such as making a staffing plan to "get through the day" given who is there and who has called in or to share information such as drug, supply, or infection warnings or reminders. At the same time, these sorts of huddles tend to happen on their own anyways, but differentiating the "LDM problem solving" that we will be discussing from these "traditional" huddles is critical. And as mentioned earlier, being able to differentiate these two when building a LDM system is critical in helping staff to understand the significance and that it is not just "one more thing" for them to do. LDM problem solving and LDM boards are the best way for them to truly "own" their work and processes and help address the problems that have plagued them for so long.

The problem solving LDM boards are anything but "wallpaper" when they are up and functioning! They are vibrant and "alive" in a department and are a visual indication of the successes, current focus, and next steps of a team.

They begin to "expand" over time and take the place of standing monthly and department meetings, e-mails, long-standing teams that never seem to accomplish anything, ad hoc "can I talk to you for 5 minutes" discussions that turn into hour-long discussions, etc. LDM boards begin to embed themselves into the "DNA" of the department and organization, and begin to reflect true cultural change, that is, they become "the way we do things around here!"

The defining characteristics of LDM problem solving and LDM boards is that they are focused solely on improvement and problem solving, not the conveyance of static or "operational" information (which is the norm with traditional boards in hospitals, as well as traditional operational "huddles")! This difference is profound and can take some time to "get right," but when it starts working, the difference is significant. Instead of staff huddling and discussing "how we will survive the day," they are instead talking about "how will we make tomorrow better than today!"

One of the core Lean wastes is "not utilizing employee creativity," where the talent, innate problem-solving ability, creativity, experience, dedication, and passion of our staff is almost completely neglected and marginalized. We have a culture where the focus of the staff is on just "doing the work" and "surviving the day" (the focus of traditional huddles and static Boards), which results in wasting all of the creativity of our staff. They "put their heads down" and get through the day, and the extent of their creativity being applied is through development of elaborate work-arounds to the broken systems and processes around them, which over time accumulate like a calcification, until the truly efficient and effective process potential underlying it is almost completely obscured.

These work-arounds are the only way that staffs in their current management system can "survive the day," and it makes for a very unpleasant experience. Most staffs go home at the end of the day extremely exhausted by the countless frustrations and "time wasters" they experienced throughout the day. The best analogy to describe this is "death by 1000 paper-cuts" or "being pecked to death by a duck." This paints a very bleak picture of how we are utilizing our staff—"surviving the day," developing work-arounds, and struggling to meet increasing workloads, decreasing resources, all while dealing with "1000 paper-cuts a day."

This "current state" of most healthcare organization's management system (or lack thereof) is why true "LDM problem solving" and engaging our staff in a fundamentally different way are absolutely critical. With staff representing approximately 80% of the operational costs of most hospitals, neglecting this tremendous resource is not only disrespectful to our staff, but it is also bad business! By changing or adding a strong "problem solving" focus to our healthcare organizations huddling process, staff can begin to focus their creativity on fixing the root causes of problems rather than using it for creating work-arounds to problems. Staff can start to remove some of the "1000 paper-cuts" that cause them to go home exhausted at the end of the day and that get in the way of providing great patient care.

You may ask "I understand the importance of problem solving, but we already do that in teams and meetings, and why does it have to be on a board?" It is a perfectly valid question. First of all, if the current approach to problem solving (meetings and teams) is working, are we making great progress? Most organizations and staff would say "no" and they would say that these meetings have poor attendance, spend most of the time with circular conversations with no ending, spend much of the time reviewing the previous meeting, and go on endlessly with no measurable impact.

One of the reasons for the lack of effectiveness for these teams and meetings is that the meetings are infrequent, without any real structure to the problem solving, and that the knowledge and next steps are spread across the team members' minds, notes, documents on computers, and elsewhere in the organization. Therefore, nobody has a full picture of where the team is, where it is going, and who is accountable for what.

A visual problem-solving LDM board addresses this, by having frequent board reviews and supporting leader rounds to establish new habits (which results in a localized culture change; it becomes "the way we do things around here" near the LDM board), a structure for meaningful problem solving (based on the A3 problem-solving approach), a central location with consensus building on the problem and measurement, a visual representation of the root cause analysis (which also works toward consensus building), and a posting of action items and its accompanying accountability. Therefore, the aspects of traditional management system problem solving (meetings and teams) are addressed with this LDM board approach.

The "visual" aspect of LDM boards deserves some attention itself, as it is key to effective organizational function. When traditional meetings occur the cadence of the meeting is for one person to talk and then the next, it is often more of a debate that is devoid of any underlying structure or discipline, where often the "loudest voice wins." There is rarely a unified direction and consensus of the team, because everybody's impression of where the team is and where it is going is dependent of their opinion, which is why these teams do not often make much progress and just "drift." When teams are all focused on a problem-solving LDM board with an embedded (simplified) A3 problem-solving structure, there is a fundamentally different team dynamic. Rather than a debate where "the loudest voice wins," the team is focused on the board instead of looking at each other, so they are all looking at the same thing. Let us pause for a moment, as this is a profound difference! By focusing on the board, they are building consensus and focusing on data and root cause analysis and clearly defined action items rather than debate and opinion! Also, many meetings can become "heated debates" where people feel attacked and minimalized. It's often a case of who can be the loudest and speak the most confidently, rather than who has the best idea, best data, or most meaningful insight. Therefore, LDM board problem solving focuses the team away from a "me versus you" structure to a "we" structure where everybody focuses on the same problem on the same place on the wall. When somebody has an idea or data, it is not just described verbally, it is reflected on the LDM board for all to see. This builds consensus and drives a different type of discussion.

The team is physically all standing in front of the same board looking at the same thing. Anybody who walks by can see the state of the team and whether or not they are functioning and progressing, and potentially step in to help if need be.

Also, with leadership rounds (which will be discussed more later), the visual nature of the boards allows senior leaders (grand rounds) to physically walk through the organization and "see" how healthy the LDM system is, how teams are progressing, and how leaders can help these teams. Just think about the significance of this—senior leaders now have a very tangible and visible way to walk through their organization and get a very accurate, objective, and meaningful understanding of which teams are functioning well and making great progress, and which are not. It is also a highly effective way of seeing which of the organizations leaders, directors, and supervisors are truly embracing the management system and driving positive and productive change in their organization, and which are floundering or using the problem solving LDM boards inappropriately and may need help or coaching. The LDM boards become the "visible artifact" of culture change in the organization, and a highly effective indicator of the health of the management system.

Therefore, LDM boards are fundamental in managing in a different way and truly engaging our staff and creating a cultural shift. At an organization's front-line unit level, we are looking to have the LDM boards drive daily-A3 team thinking on small to medium-sized problems (with larger more strategic problems being addressed through value stream map (VSM), Kaizen events, strategic/enterprise A3s, etc., which are identified and initiated through the LDM board escalation process that we will discuss later). Fundamentally, as long as the teams are following A3 thinking on a regular (ideally daily) cadence, then the exact structure of the LDM board is not critical. But like with most forms of teaching and learning, structure is important in teaching the discipline and having a structure that supports the thought process and discipline. Also, the leader rounding process (introduced and discussed later) is supported by a consistent structure. As leaders gain familiarity with a consistent structure to the boards they can visually see the thought process, progress, gaps, and other items (such as escalation items) when rounding and can therefore more effectively engage with the teams. Therefore, even though the "spirit of the law" is more important than the "letter of the law" with LDM boards to drive A3 thinking, to have consistency and a management system that extends beyond a single board or department, the structure should be substantially (but not completely) consistent between boards, levels, and areas. This is not to say that the boards need to be (or even should be) carbon copies of a rigid template. Department to department variation in work content, variability, confidentiality, nature of problems, and problems the teams encounter will necessitate some customization of their boards to ensure the process is effective. A modest level of customization drives more local ownership of the boards. This customization of the boards usually comes with time, practice, and figuring out the boards. Once teams "get it," they know enough about the structure, cadence, and the "why" behind the "what" to allow them to customize in a meaningful way without sacrificing the systematic nature of the LDM boards.

If leaders and staff tried to customize LDM boards extensively in the beginning, it would likely compromise the future success of the boards. The following discussion will describe the essential aspects and suggested form of the LDM boards and their terminology, which are a solid foundation to start with. Your organization might want to customize the terminology or other aspects from the very beginning to address particular "sensitivities" or other initiatives within your program, but keep the framework intact because it aligns closely with "timeless and proven" principles such as A3, scientific method and plan-do-study-act (PDSA).

Fundamentally, the LDM board follows a simplified A3 structure, and is meant to drive daily A3 thinking. With an A3 form and A3 thinking/problem solving, one of the primary goals is to "slow down" the thought process and drive a more methodical, stepwise, thoughtful approach to problem solving. The natural human instinct when encountering a perceived problem is to "jump to conclusions" and immediately start solving for the problem. This "bad habit" is not only ineffective; it is actually counterproductive and even destructive to organizations! Without taking the time to clearly understand the problem, understand the current process, and verify root causes, the countermeasures are determined solely based upon assumption, conjecture, and opinion. This often leads to countermeasures/action items being implemented that don't actually solve the problem, or aim to solve a problem that doesn't exist. This then can lead to additional steps being added to a process, resources being expended, and divisiveness between teams, due to another destructive habit of teams doing problem solving "focusing on people, not process!"

Common phrases surrounding this dysfunctional dynamic are "if only Fred would do his job!" or "Susie NEVER does that!" These assumptions and dysfunctions usually lead to punitive, accusatory, or regulatory actions that add workload, usually aren't followed, and add complexity and division but definitely not the management system that we want to have! This is a distinct characteristic of the "default management system" that was mentioned earlier.

To avoid these "bad habits of team problem solving," the LDM board process follows a simplified A3 thought process. On an A3, there are two distinct sides. The left-hand side of the A3 form focuses on clearly identifying and exploring the problem and identifying and verifying root causes but not on countermeasures or actions! This teaches teams to not skip the most critical parts of problem solving and generate "destructive" or counterproductive ideas that add complexity to the system. The right-hand side of the A3 is focused on the future state of the process, an implementation plan, estimating impact, etc. The critical part of the right-hand side of the A3 form is that you don't go there too early! We usually tell our students to fold the A3 form in half and not even look at the right-hand side of the form. The future process and countermeasures on an A3 are not targeted at addressing the problem statement on the left-hand side of the A3 even though this might seem counterintuitive. The future process and countermeasures are targeted at solving the root causes of the problem statement! If we solve for the problem statement directly, we are "jumping to the right-hand side" and potentially (and very likely) solving for many more of the contributing factors of the problem than there are actually primary drivers of the problem.

You are remembered for the rules you break.

–Douglas MacArthur

Therefore, a simplified version of the A3 would be (1) clear identification of the problem and identification of the "gap" between where we are and where we want to be (the top half of the left-hand side of an A3), (2) root cause analysis and validation of the actual primary root causes (to get the maximum impact with the minimum amount of actions and to not add complexity to the system) and (3) countermeasures/action plan to address the primary root causes of the problem (right-hand side of the A3). This simplified A3 three-layer structure will be the basic framework of our LDM boards.

In addition to this core problem-solving structure, there are several other aspects of an LDM board that are critical. During the LDM problem-solving process, there are occasionally problems that are bigger, more complicated, multi-departmental, compliance or risk related, or some other type of issue that cannot be solved at the local LDM board. These sorts of issues require a corner of the board to be designated as "escalation items," which will link closely with the senior leader "grand rounds" or other leader rounds. When rounding, the leaders know that this is "their corner" and they can take these items, evaluate, and work on them, and then report back to the team (see Figure 3.1).

The other section of the LDM board (and it is sometimes its own board) is what we call "operational LDM boards" or "project management/ prioritization LDM boards" and they take on a different structure between front-line LDM boards and higher level LDM boards. We will discuss the front-line board first, and then the higher-level board.

For the front-line "operational LDM board," there is a unique opportunity and approach to "kick off" the huddling process in a way that engages the what's-in-it-for-me (WIIFM) principle for the front-line staff: What's-in-it-for-me! One of the primary forms of pushback you will get when trying to start LDM boards with front-line staff is that "we don't have enough time!" Therefore, a natural first step would be to focus the LDM board initially (and throughout its life) on "how can we give time back to staff?"

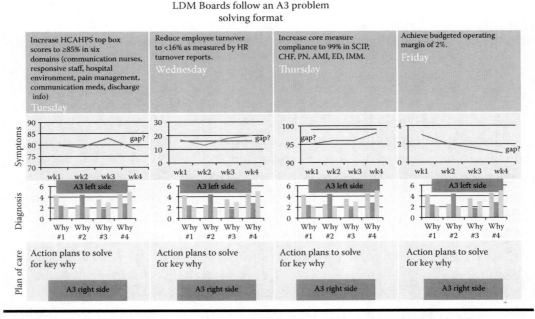

Figure 3.1   **LDM board with similar structure to A3 (left- and right-hand sides).**

Therefore, having a section of the board for "time wasters and frustrations" is highly effective to start engaging the teams. With this section, you ask the staff "what gets in the way of you doing your job?" and "what are your time wasters and frustrations?" and usually the ideas start flooding in. These ideas range from simple things that the leader and staff can implement (just-do-its or simple things that don't require analysis and are relatively simple and cheap to implement), small- to medium-sized problems that would be a perfect start to the LDM board (setting our LDM board up for success with this kickoff discussion!), to large VSM or system-wide problems that will need to be escalated. By engaging the staff with this at first, the what's in it for me (WIIFM) principle is addressed. The team already has some small wins associated with the LDM board, and there are some escalation items that the leaders can take and "run with" and engage with their teams in a constructive way.

For supervisors, middle level and senior managers, they generally have less of a need for addressing "time wasters and frustrations" and more of a need for project management and prioritization (which isn't generally needed at the front-line level).

For these groups, having a simple 2 × 2 matrix with axis of "high/low urgency and importance" or "high/low difficulty and impact" provides a meaningful framework for overloaded managers and leaders to take what is "in their head" and put it on their LDM board. Feedback from most groups that do this is that it is very cathartic and helpful in managing the numerous projects and initiatives. Teams can use this board to balance and coordinate work and priorities. Each staff member or group has a unique color of post-it™ notes to add additional visibility to who is working on what, how to balance or shift work to help each other out, etc. An additional benefit of this sort of board is that it drives a more meaningful discussion with a manager or leader who you report to. People often talk about how busy they are or how many things they have going on and how overwhelmed they are, but this is often just "white noise" to a senior leader. They hear this from everybody and are essentially tone-deaf to it. When a senior leader looks at the operational LDM board (see Figure 3.2) of one of their direct reports and sees all of the tasks/projects/initiatives laid out on a framework of urgency and importance, it drives a whole different discussion. Just like we mentioned earlier with the LDM board, when the discussion is focused on a LDM board instead of a "me versus you" discussion, it tends to objectify the discussion in a meaningful and more productive way, rather than a "standoff of wills" or who has the louder voice.

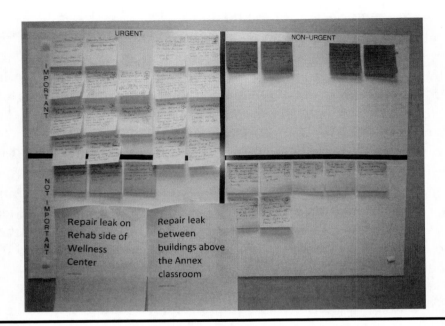

Figure 3.2   Picture of 2 × 2 LDM board priority matrix.

In addition to helping with personal management and management of tasks in teams, LDM boards also fill a critical gap in many Lean transformations.

When a team works on a small, medium, or large project and the project doesn't get implemented or implemented successfully, it is rarely the result of the team not coming up with good ideas or a good plan that would work. Most often, the project fails due to a lack of leader engagement, project management, or just implementing the changes that were identified by the team. Therefore, this operational prioritization LDM board tool helps to instill basic project management skills in teams, and makes the project management of teams (or lack thereof) more visible to leaders. Also, the LDM board structure for problem solving is extremely complimentary in function to the operational LDM board, as action items can and do flow between these boards, and can also be a highly effective tool for managing large and small projects.

Returning to the discussion of the three sections of the LDM board (the simplified A3 structure), we need to briefly discuss some critical semantics that may seem like a minor detail, but the subtleties are profound. Traditional ways to label the three sections are to label the top section as a "run chart," the middle section as "analysis," and the bottom section as "action plans."

These are completely accurate and descriptive terms for the purpose and use of each section, so there is no fault with this structure. The fault comes down to the natural human and team instinct to jump to conclusions and start generating action items before the problem is well defined at all, and usually completely skipping the critical analysis section. Without the analysis and getting to some sort of root cause based on defensible data or analysis, the LDM board problem-solving process is just a visual version of the same dysfunctional problem solving that is the "default management system" of most organizations. When teaching students about the LDM board process, the criticality of the analysis section was stressed to the point of exhaustion, with almost endless reinforcement. Despite this, it was almost universally skipped during the first several iterations of implementing the LDM boards in an area and required very direct feedback to the teams pointing out the huge gap in the middle of their LDM board (when they did follow the structure, which wasn't always the case at first). This seems perplexing because many of these staff were healthcare professionals such as doctors, nurses, physician assistants/nurse practitioners, techs, etc., and they had been taught diagnostic techniques for identifying and treating illness! With the LDM board problems, we are doing exactly the same thing as treating patients, except applying those same principles to processes that are "sick" and where we don't know what is causing the illness. That is, the problem is really a (1) "symptom" that we want to alleviate by identifying the root cause through (2) diagnosis and implementing an appropriate (3) treatment plan. If we treated patients the same way we treat processes and skipped the diagnosis, then we would be developing treatment plans to treat their symptoms rather than identifying and addressing the true underlying condition.

Therefore, a fundamental gap with the LDM boards was to help the staff to apply the knowledge and thought process they already possessed and had refined over years of experience and education in patient care to the LDM board process. What a tremendous resource! This is yet another example of the fundamental Lean waste of "not utilizing employee creativity" we already have a healthcare organization or hospital full of trained problem solvers, but we need to figure out how to engage their clinical minds in process and operational problem solving!

To illustrate this gap, we ask the staff and providers what they would do if a patient came to the hospital with a horrific, splitting headache where he or she could barely see or walk? As they begin to answer and talk about how they would run imaging and blood tests, I would rudely interrupt and say that we would give them an *acetaminophen* and send them on their way! The class would then look perplexed, confused, and a little annoyed. Then I would smile and explain that I was just illustrating a critical point that skipping analysis is exactly like giving a patient who potentially has a more serious condition an *acetaminophen* and that we need to apply the same level of rigor to our problem-solving process. We would then have a little brainstorming session about what could be causing the headache, and they usually say a tumor, aneurism, stroke, concussion, hangover, etc. and that to rule each of these out would require specific investigation and diagnosis, and then we could develop a treatment plan.

With this analogy in place, numerous clinicians and staff had said, "Now I get it! It didn't 'click' until you put it in those terms"! With this in mind, we started adding this terminology to the LDM board in all healthcare organizations we work with. The top layer is a "symptom," the middle layer is "diagnosis," and the bottom layer is "treatment plan" (see Figure 3.3).

Before delving into each of these three layers individually, it is a good moment to stress another key point of the LDM board process, that is, "neatness" and "pretty" are not associated with an effective LDM board, and this also leads into a discussion about the "LDM board life cycle." Most LDM boards follow a pattern similar to this: The staff member learns about LDM boards through training and goes back very enthused to start. They grab every cool looking chart and graph they can find and tape them to the LDM board. There is very little structure or order to it, and it takes a huge amount of effort to create. After 3 or 4 months, you look at the board, and the dates on the pieces of paper are all 3 or 4 months old, it is just wallpaper! There is no structure to it, it didn't drive problem solving, it took a huge amount of effort to set up, and then it wasn't maintained or used. We call this "building to impress." After providing feedback to the team, they tear it down and start from scratch, with a very narrow focus and just practicing the discipline. After several more cycles of experimentation with the LDM board, and tearing it down and building it up again, as well as practicing the LDM problem-solving sessions, the team finally "gets it," and the final functional LDM board looks kind of crude, but the dates on action items and data are current, ideas are being generated, and it is a meaningful and productive use of staff's' time. Therefore, what impresses a LDM board coach is the opposite of what people think; it is when it is a "living/breathing" board that is truly engaging the staff when the LDM board coach gets excited, not when there are lots of fancy charts and graphs (which the lay person might be impressed with). Just like A3s should be done with pencil and eraser because they are living documents,

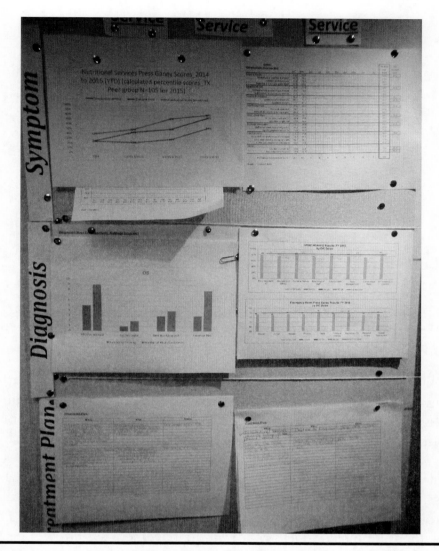

Figure 3.3   Picture of LDM board with (1) symptoms, (2) diagnosis, and (3) treatment plan.

so should the LDM board. A collection of post-it notes, colored markers and highlighters, and pencils and erasers should be in close proximity (see Figure 3.4).

Just adding a single dot to a graph to update is much easier than pulling up a spreadsheet, adding another data point to it, printing it off, and posting it on the board. Also, there is a certain amount of comparative analysis and trending that naturally takes place when a human puts a data point on a chart. Is it going up or down? Are our action items driving this in the right direction? Another critical point is that when LDM boards become a

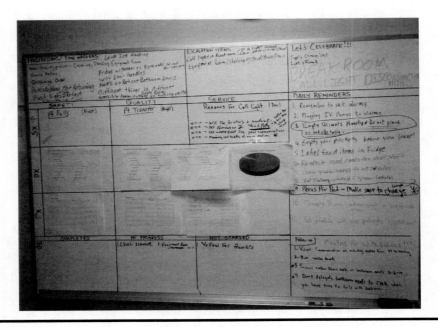

Figure 3.4 Picture of LDM board (in development).

competition of who can have the prettiest and most impressive board, then not only are staff wasting a lot of time, they are also putting peer pressure on others. Staff who aren't good with computers will feel excluded or intimidated from the process, which is precisely what we don't want! In our experience, some of the best problem solvers are those who don't have extensive computer skills. One of the many attributes of a meaningful Lean management system is that it is inclusive and you can engage staff at all levels and in all roles. If we create a wasteful and competitive process around LDM boards, then the inclusiveness of a Lean management system will be lost and this will severely compromise future efforts.

Now, onto a "deeper dive" into the details of the three major sections of an LDM board, as well as the subsections and other components of the LDM board:

■ *Headers:* Headers are one of the permanent sections that go at the top of the board; Common approaches to defining the headers are to use Toyota's Safety Quality Delivery Cost and Morale (SQDCM) or "pillar" goals of your organization, or any other meaningful strategic or operational set of categories that provide the proper context for a "balanced scorecard" approach to working on improvement opportunities.

Sometimes groups make the mistake of feeling compelled to have all of the categories listed, and then "stretch" to come up with things to work on that fall under the categories. This is not a good way to go! Over time, we want the LDM process to become more and more meaningful, and feeling like we need to "fit a square peg in a round hole" will not be good for the future health of the LDM problem-solving process. If you are in the finance department and there is not a good safety topic, then don't have this in your LDM board header! These categories will also help to define the "cadence" of your daily board reviews. For example, on a nursing unit, every Monday review may be on safety, every Tuesday on quality, Wednesday on delivery, Thursday on cost, and discuss morale on Friday). These categories therefore aren't just labels and they allow you to set the cadence of the boards to allow enough time to research root causes, gather data, and implement action items. If teams are conducting board reviews more often than they are generating ideas or gathering data to help them more clearly understand the problem, then there is a disconnect that needs to be addressed.

■ *Symptom:* Just like the problem statement at the top of an A3, we want to be able to quantify the "gap" between where we are (baseline) and where we want to be (goal). Teams sometimes don't want to take the time to quantify this, because they are so sure that it is a problem and seem to see this as an extra step or slowing them down. There are two reasons why this is counterproductive. If the team is wildly successful with the improvement, they then can't say how much of an improvement it is and just end saying "it feels better." Therefore, the success and celebration is muted.

The second reason LDM symptoms are critical is there is a tremendous potential opportunity being skipped; the perceived problem might not actually be a problem! Helping a team discover that a perceived problem is not a real problem is one of the most desired outcomes of an A3, and the same is the case with a LDM board. If you skip this step of quantifying the problem and the gap, then diagnosis becomes extremely difficult or impossible, and we start defaulting to our old mode of problem solving. Also, as mentioned earlier, drawing this by hand is highly preferable to a fancy computer chart or graph. Using a simple piece of graph paper with 1–31 listed on the bottom (for days of the month) is a highly effective approach for making it simple to draw and update the chart by hand and get usable and clear information from it.

■ *Diagnosis:* As mentioned earlier, Diagnosis is one of the most critical and most commonly skipped sections! Due to this, we highly recommend having lines demarcating the three sections (symptoms, diagnosis, and treatment plan) of the LDM board and encouraging content to be in its appropriate section. This draws attention to teams "skipping a step" so that they can be coached and supported in following the proper process. For the diagnosis section, teams can use their creativity in how to do the diagnosis. Pareto analysis is often a highly effective tool for looking for the 80/20-principle that usually 20% of the causes are causing 80% of the problems. We encourage teams to use "dots on a page," basically just a simple approach to "counting" the frequency, distribution, severity, and any other patterns that could be helpful in the root cause analysis (see Figure 3.5).

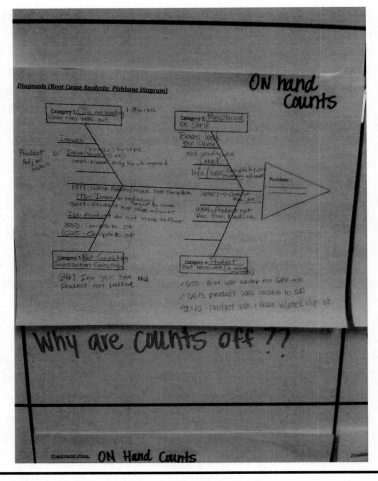

Figure 3.5 Picture of LDM board with diagnosis section.

While it might not immediately seem like a tool for root cause analysis, "going to the Gemba" is actually the most effective tool for root cause analysis! The "Gemba" is a Japanese term that equates to "where the work takes place." While many people (especially more analytical staff who may be drawn to approaches such as Six Sigma, benchmarking, or other similar sources of data) may see this as a wasteful or unnecessary aspect of root cause analysis, it is really a form of error-proofing as well, which we will explore next.

We often ask students "which of these three is the most reliable," and then point to our mouth (what we say or what others say), ears (what we hear or perceive from others), and eyes (what we see firsthand) and then discuss these in sequence. "Do the words we say or that others speak to us sometimes deceive us?" Universally they say yes. "Does what we hear or how we perceive what is told to us reflect reality?" Again, they say yes. "When we take the time to go and look and observe (go to the Gemba") without interfering and see what is actually happening, does this usually deceive us?" At this point, they usually agree that this is the most reliable approach. For our students, therefore, we regularly point to our eyes and remind them to "go to the Gemba and see what is actually taking place," not what we hear, perceive, or assume.

Why do you think that what we hear, speak, and/or perceive when we listen to others is regularly divergent from reality?

A critical piece of this is the phenomenon of "expectation bias" (Rosenthal, 1966). This is a phenomenon where our brains anticipate a certain outcome or series of events based on a specific set of initial conditions. Magicians often take advantage of this expectation bias or hard-wired mental processes to trick our minds to see an outcome that we didn't expect to see (hence the perceived "magic"). Most managers were promoted "through the ranks" due to their technical expertise, training, and experience. As they become managers, they usually separate themselves from much of the day-to-day technical work, but in their mind they still assume that the technical work or processes still proceed exactly the way they did it, and that others do it the same way. The more time that passes, the farther their "mental model" of the work diverges from reality, as time, technology, regulation, process variability, and other environmental factors surrounding the work evolve. They interpret the world and processes around them according to this model, and they don't necessarily perceive what is going on, just what they expect to be going on (by interpreting what they perceive in a biased way).

This divergence from reality extends to data as well, as does the bad habit of assuming what the process, data, or other input "means" what the superficial or "expected" interpretation says that it means. For example, one of the first projects I ever worked on in a hospital involved patient-flow data, so just like any other newly minted engineer, I dove into the data set with abandon and started looking for patterns, which I definitely found, especially in one of the data fields. As I continued the analysis, I ended up going and talking to a floor nurse to learn more about what I was seeing, and I am glad I did! This nurse told me (and showed me) that the data field that I was trying to analyze was actually a required field to get to more meaningful parts of the electronic medical record, so nurses just put dummy-data in to get to the next section. Needless to say, this data was absolutely worthless! The reality of the situation came from "going to the Gemba" and not using this faulty data in any root cause analysis or related work.

For this reason, we again recommend very simple and direct data gathering using the "dots on a page" approach to data collection. When we can fully depend on data sets or automatically collected data, then by all means use this data, but only if you and the team understand and believe in the data. I often see teams problem solving on patient satisfaction data with arbitrary goals, and the teams are trying to understand patterns and other aspects of the data to try to figure out how to improve. As I work with these teams, I usually ask whether the scores are "top box," percentiles, mean, median, etc., and the teams usually don't know. I direct them to "take a step back" and understand what and where the data they are interpreting, to be careful with "lagging indicators," and understand what and where the scores come from to know how to interpret them. With a "dots on a page" approach, we recommend that teams look for "countable" events or data points that they can count on a daily or weekly basis, and then come back to the LDM board to update. This approach has three distinct advantages: (1) the data that is gathered is real-time (or close to real time), (2) because it is just "counts" it isn't time consuming, and (3) the staff are the ones gathering the data, so they have knowledge, belief, and trust in the data (rather than arguing that the data set from the computer doesn't reflect reality).

With the "dots on a page" approach (see Figure 3.6), the astute team member often asks "how many or how long do I need to gather this to be significant?" We respond in the following way: "We are not writing an

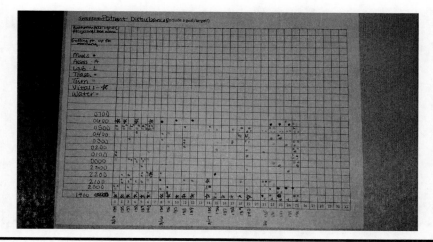

Figure 3.6   Picture of "dots on a page" informal LDM data collection technique.

academic or medical journal article on this, so there is no inherent need for statistical significance or other level of rigor. We need a data set that is large enough for some degree of confidence (such as a sample size of 25 to assume a normal distribution), and that represents a relatively normal day/week/month. If we gather data for a shorter period of time, but the period of time is representative of a relatively average period of time, then we have good enough baseline data that can be used for baseline measurements and root cause analysis. If the period of time is 'abnormal' for some reason, then we need to gather more."

The power of this simple "dots on a page" measurement is also that it is nonlabor intensive, thus lending itself to "after" validation, and periodic monitoring of the process once it has been improved and standardized. The "dots on a page" approach is empowering for any staff member and doesn't require advanced statistic knowledge or analytics, and this empowering of root cause analysis and data gathering throughout a healthcare system is absolutely critical. It is intimately tied to "the Gemba" and engaging the creativity and problem solving of our staff, and is therefore central to what we are trying to achieve.

For the manager working on root-cause analysis (diagnosis) in an LDM board, the criticality of "going to the Gemba" is just as powerful, as it helps re-sync their perception/mental-model with reality.

But you must remember that "Going to the Gemba" requires a high degree of humility and stepping back from your role as a manager. When "Going to the Gemba," try to be as unobtrusive as possible, and just watch the process and see what you see. If you see a staff member doing something that they shouldn't, don't intervene (unless, of course, there is risk to patient safety or some other critical issue), just observe the process as being "what it is."

> *Every system is perfectly designed to achieve the results it gets.*
>
> **–Frederick Winslow Taylor**

That is, you are seeing what the process is—not what it should, shouldn't, or could be. By gathering this data and observation of the true reality of the process by neutrally observing, our understanding of the true process is grounded in reality and not biased by expectation, mental-models, or other issues that cloud the situation. This alignment is a powerful tool for root cause analysis that often yields significant benefits.

One of the most powerful of these benefits is that a problem often goes up on the LDM board because it is perceived as happening "all the time" or "somebody never does their job." During the data gathering process and root cause analysis, a common conclusion is that "this problem isn't actually a problem," and it comes off of the LDM board. This has three primary benefits: (1) It reinforces the criticality of "going to the Gemba" and the power of the process to the team. (2) It saves the effort that would have been expended on solving a problem that wasn't actually a problem. (3) It avoided actual "process degradation" that would have occurred from adding processes, policies, or steps to solve a problem that wasn't a problem, thus adding waste and complexity to the overall system.

Another form of diagnosis is also important to explore. It is critical to quantify the "symptom" of the problem, as it is difficult to make an argument that it is actually a problem if there is no possible way to quantify it. Sometimes (rarely), even for problems (symptoms) that we have quantified a "gap," it can prove extremely challenging to quantify the root causes and come up with primary root causes (diagnosis) to focus our action items (treatment plan) due to limitations of sample size, frequency (such as sentinel events), lack of an "audit trail," or other similar factors. Given the extreme emphasis placed on the significance of "diagnosis" to link the "symptom" to the "treatment plan," teams can see this as an impassable barrier.

While it is ideal for numerical data to justify the focus on specific root causes as key drivers, the ultimate goal is to positively impact the "symptom" metric and use the scientific method. To progress through the process and continue with the scientific method, it is critical to find a path forward and come up with a "hypothesis" to try and see if it will positively impact the metric. In the absence of effectively quantifiable data, other approaches must be explored to help the team progress.

One of these approaches can be the "Gemba" approach previously described, which may provide actionable insights to narrow in on a treatment plan for the problem. For example, if there is such a high degree of process variability that it is clearly evident that every staff member follows a different process, this can be challenging to quantify. At the same time, this knowledge is highly actionable due to the criticality of establishing a stable process to even begin having the opportunity to improve the process (Standard work is in the foundation of the Toyota house.).

> *Where there is no standard there can be no Kaizen.*

> **–Taiichi Ohno**

Once there is a fundamental understanding of the "foundational principles" of Lean such as the need for standard work, it is not hard to come to the conclusion that a lack of LDM boards or standard work are causing the problem. A qualitative or "assessment" approach to the foundation of the Toyota house as it relates to the process could be sufficient for some of the critical initial treatment plan action items to be identified and initiated. Without this fundamental understanding of Lean foundational principles by the team, the leader will need to guide the team (through the Socratic method) to help them understand the significance of this "gap," but over time these "foundational principles" should be easy (and safe!) for the team to "jump to" in the treatment plan.

Another qualitative approach that can be used to help teams bridge this gap (with a lack of quantification for root cause analysis) is a qualitative "consensus building" or "expert opinion" approach to prioritizing the root causes. One approach would be the teams using a voting technique to come to a consensus of where to focus their countermeasure efforts. These approaches would allow the team to "narrow" their focus, which is critical, and to progress to the point of being able to test their hypothesis. Even if the teams' narrowing was incorrect, the results of their "experiment" will provide an effective feedback loop to go back to the root cause analysis, challenge their assumptions and expert opinions, and re-evaluate what their next experiment will be. This iterative approach, despite being qualitative, is a form of a heuristic that allows for the team to iteratively identify hypotheses, test these hypotheses, and usually narrow in on the counter-measures that will result in moving their metrics in the correct direction.

Another method for executing this approach would be to develop a scoring mechanism to evaluate and rank the potential root causes. This adds additional rigor to the qualitative assessment of the potential root causes. For example, the different potential root causes could be ranked according to difficulty, impact, urgency, risk, cost, speed of implementation, or other factors. This scoring could be done right on the fishbone diagram or the 5-whys diagram and then show a tangible connection with why specific root causes are being addressed in the treatment plan.

With teams hopefully "lingering" in the diagnosis section until there is a sufficiently high level of confidence and rigor, they are ready to proceed to the "treatment plan" section of the LDM board, which is the first opportunity to truly address the symptom and hopefully move the metrics in the right direction!

■ *Treatment Plan:* Even though we heavily emphasized the importance of the diagnosis section of the LDM board, without identifying and implementing action items (treatment plan), the problems/metrics we are trying to impact will not move unless we do some experiments and make changes to hopefully address the root causes! Even though the treatment plan section might seem pretty straightforward compared to the symptom and diagnosis sections, there are still a variety of critical considerations to keep in mind.

The treatment plan is, at its most basic level, the actions or steps necessary to address the actionable primary root causes and to test the team's "hypothesis."

While at its most basic level, this is an accurate description; the action plan needs to include a number of other important consider-ations to be effective. As with any change, there needs to be a number of change-management considerations added, such as building con-sensus with other affected areas, obtaining approvals when necessary, educating other staff members, doing small tests of change before full deployment, evaluating unintended effects on other processes, poten-tially obtaining resources or physical changes necessary to implement, data gathering to measure the impact (or lack thereof) of the change, as well as other actions.

Another important consideration is to avoid "bundling" of action items on your treatment plan, such as listing very large items to implement. If one lists "implement new registration process," this larger action item encompasses probably 10 separate sub-items, and it will be difficult for the team to ever be able to "check-off" this action item. This causes two separate problems: (1) as leaders round and look at LDM boards, they wonder why action items are not being completed or implemented and (2) it is very motivating for teams to feel and see their progress and see action items being "checked off," which is very difficult when they are bundled into large items and rarely checked off.

Therefore, the "treatment plan" (see Figure 3.7) needs to be a detailed: (1) what, (2) who, and (3) when to conduct the experiment on addressing the primary root causes, taking into consideration some level of granular detail that also includes holistic considerations of affected parties, change management, communication, approvals, and regulation.

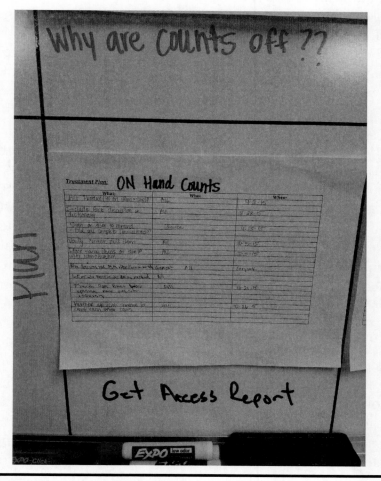

Figure 3.7   LDM "treatment plan."

Once the team has gotten to the point of identifying actionable items on their treatment plan, the focus shifts to implementing these counter-measures. As mentioned previously, we want these tasks/action items to be as granular as possible to allow the team to "check them off" and motivate the team, as well as demonstrate progress to any of the leaders that round on the board. As the team implements these action items, it is very rare that they are implemented linearly and without any surprises. This is completely normal and to be expected! As the team runs into these "surprises" it is critical to let the team know that this is absolutely normal, as they can sometimes see these as a contra-indication of the accuracy of their problem solving and investigation. The action plan is actually a perfect example of PDSA in action, with rapid-cycle experimentation, learning, modification of the root cause analysis, and action plan updating, with this iterating until the metrics begin to move and (hopefully) reach their target.

If the implementation of the action plan doesn't move the metrics (symptom) toward the goal, this is almost certainly an indication that there was a misstep with the root cause analysis (diagnosis) and that the action plan is attempting to address root causes that aren't the primary driver of the problem.

In this case, it is especially important to help the team understand that this is a "successful failure" and nothing to be discouraged about! Without this encouragement and intervention, teams can lose motivation and give up (or lose hope). Unless the team had exhaustive and unarguable data (which is ideal but rare), there is often some uncertainty (especially in healthcare with the disproportionately high rate of the "human component" of processes). This is just a very predictable and necessary example of "taking a step back." The team simply needs to back up one step to the analysis (diagnosis) section and reevaluate their assumptions and data, potentially gather additional data, and pick a different primary branch of their root cause analysis to go down. For example, they may have assumed that the primary root cause was due to technology or equipment. After addressing multiple issues with technology or equipment, the metric they were targeting to improve hasn't improved despite extensive efforts. At this point, the team would step back and ask themselves questions such as the following: "Were the staff fully trained on using the technology?" "Did we inform them of the technological changes?" "Did the technology changes have unintended consequences that created new problems?" "Are we fully using the capabilities of the current technology?" "Is there a lower-tech option, such as LDM boards, that we could experiment with earlier to try to improve the process?"

With these sorts of questions, the team goes back to the root cause analysis (diagnosis) section and has a much better understanding of the problem (due to the "successful failure" of the first attempt) and works through the process until they have enough confidence to set up a new "experiment" (treatment plan) and hopefully move their metric in the right direction.

Through this iterative PDSA cycle, they continually learn more and more about their problem, develop a greater understanding of the LDM process, and "rewire" their brains from the "firefighting" mentality that is so common in most organizations and begin the critical journey of maturing their LDM system. The role of the manager has shifted from being the "problem solver/firefighter" to being the "LDM Board leader/ facilitator" and "developer of people." Achievement of strategic and individual goals transitions from being a once-a-year focus at the individual and senior team level to being an organization-wide and team based approach that takes place continually throughout the entire year. It also signals a fundamental cultural shift, as "the way we do things around here" is reflected in a team-based, aligned, positive, A3-thinking focused approach that has problem solving and ownership occurring at its most basic level. This is truly cultural change at its most fundamental, granular, and observable level.

In addition to these three "core" sections of the LDM board, the following sections of the LDM board provide critical additive support to the core function of the LDM Board. These sections will now be explored:

■ *Escalation items:* While the teams are going through the LDM board process, they occasionally encounter potentially high-risk, critical, or other problems that are seemingly very real, but cannot (for various reasons) be solved at the LDM board. It is critical that these issues have an outlet as otherwise they "fester" for years, which is an unfortunate organizational "bad habit" that we have to break!

When these issues arise, we want to have a corner of the LDM board that allows these issues to have an outlet. As we build and reinforce the leader and senior leader rounds, the power and effectiveness of this escalation process continues to grow (see Figure 3.8). As you round through the different boards, you see where the escalation items were identified and where they ended up, and also the feedback loop to the originators (which is critical for them to understand the "why" of doing the escalation process).

This also represents a unique opportunity for the organization to manage and minimize risk according to the "iceberg" metaphor, with the "tip of the iceberg" being the sentinel events or other severe problems that come to the forefront of the organization. The usual mode is the traditional "firefighting" of senior leaders, where they react to the sentinel events or other catastrophic outcomes in normally dramatic and shortsighted ways to address the issue as

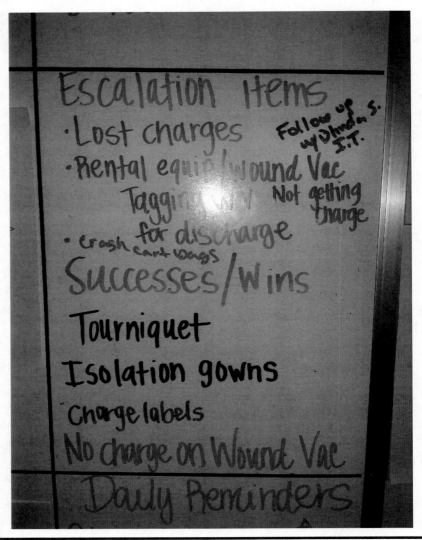

Figure 3.8 "Escalation" section LDM board.

quickly and as thoroughly as possible. Unfortunately, given that this is only the "tip of the iceberg," there is a huge portion of the iceberg that remains hidden. The sentinel or other event is the "visible" problem, the "festering" problems that don't have a mechanism such as the escalation system to bring them to the forefront to be solved. This is similar to the Lean perspective of the damaging effects of "hidden wastes" (wastes that aren't visible, but cause a multitude of problems and issues throughout the organization, and are difficult to address because they aren't visible). With the "tip of the iceberg" approach to solving problems, senior leaders let the main "bulk" of the iceberg underwater sustain and damage the organization, only to have it become visible when a potentially "worst case" scenario actually comes to reality. Of the thousands of near misses, only one actually has the ability to make itself visible. It is a dangerous, inefficient, and reactive process and way to deal with an organization.

The escalation process, in tandem with the LDM boards and helping develop our teams into effective problem solvers and who see management as proactively engaging in their LDM boards and "running with" escalation problems that are identified, presents a unique opportunity for us to use our leaders and senior leaders in the way they were meant to be used: proactively, and in a supportive and empowering way, solving problems through the "early warning system" of the organization's LDM boards. They are taking advantage of staff throughout the organization identifying risks or problems before they result in sentinel or other severe outcomes, identifying solutions in a nonreactive manner, and helping the organization plan more "offensively" (proactive) instead of "defensively" (reactive). In this system, problems don't remain hidden as long, and they become visible from the escalation system rather than through sentinel or negative events (see Figure 3.9).

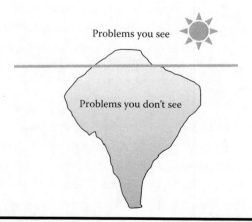

Figure 3.9   LDM "iceberg" model.

Over time, this process will incrementally decrease organizational risk, and the cultural feedback mechanism of staff seeing their leaders acting on what they escalated drives an ongoing cultural shift in a positive direction.

For the higher level and mid-management LDM boards, more space will be needed than just the "corner" of the front-line LDM boards. For these higher level management boards that will have more escalation items, a very effective structure is to have three different sections to the board that the escalation items move between: (1) not started (identified but nothing else or determined to be nonfeasible) (2) in progress (being worked on but not finalized and (3) completed. These can also be color coded as red/yellow/green (respectively).

In terms of integrating with leader and senior leader rounding, it is critical to realize that escalation items should not be an uncommon occurrence with LDM boards. If there are no escalation items on any level of LDM board consistently (over several different rounds), this is a sign that the system is not being actively used. Also, if action items are "piling up" in the not started part of the LDM board, or not getting through to completion, then this is also a sign of a problem with the system.

The final note on the escalation system is critical, and it deals with the accountability of leaders who take escalation items. If there is not follow through back to the originating team and other interested parties, then the system will not be viable. For example, if a team escalates an action item related to staffing or equipment (which shouldn't be escalation items in mature systems, because they are solutions, not problems) that is not affordable within the organization, a clear and honest explanation must be returned to the originating LDM board. It must be clear and evident to the team that leadership took the escalation item seriously, looked into it, and invested time and energy on it, and then had honesty and integrity to tell them the truth even if it is not what they wanted to hear. Otherwise, they see the escalation items as being a "black box" that doesn't go anywhere and is a waste of time.

- *Frustrations/time wasters (front-line boards):* A mature LDM board will have a variety of different metrics, many of which are closely aligned with overall organizational goals, as well as mirror and reflect many aspects of a Hoshin planning (refer to Chapter 6) approach being used for strategy deployment. Please note that this is for a "mature" LDM board, which takes time to set up and mature, which is not where we start!

When starting an LDM board, the primary focus IS NOT on impacting the metrics or even having demonstrable successes! This may seem counterintuitive given the overall intent of the LDM system, but let's explore this further.

The analogy of "Give a man a fish, he eats for a day. Teach a man to fish, and he eats for a lifetime" applies here. As with most aspects of Lean/total productive maintenance (TPM), our primary focus is on developing individuals, teams, leaders, and the overall organization. When beginning to manage LDM Boards, our primary focus is on establishing the discipline, changing the behaviors, and learning to think and problem solve differently.

Given these facts, when we are first starting to develop and manage LDM Boards, teams can be intimidated by the structure, discipline, and results of more mature LDM Boards and not know where to begin. They can sometimes try to mimic the more mature LDM Boards and tackle problems the way these teams are, which can be very difficult due to their different maturity levels. Therefore, we need to "meet them where they are" and help pick some "practice problems," which might seem almost trivial or overly simple to go on an LDM board. But these simple problems are great opportunities for the teams to practice and get some "small wins."

To help populate the LDM boards for these "practice problems" and for future issues to put on the LDM boards, it is very helpful to have a section of the LDM board for "time wasters and frustrations." This is exactly what it sounds like: What are the time wasters that take up too much of your day and the frustrations that you feel are getting in the way of you doing your job? When you try to start teams off with highly aligned or strategic goals, they often give you a "deer in the headlights" look and then feel like they are just being asked to solve administration's problems and that there is no WIIFM. If you start out with "time wasters and frustrations," then they have a strong understanding of WIIFM and begin to see this as "their" board instead of "administration's" board. These time wasters and frustrations are absolutely critical for kicking off the LDM boards, but it is also helpful in a mature/"steady state" LDM board. It basically functions as a queue for a mixed assortment of issues to be identified and captured. Some of these many issues become escalation items, others will be just-do-its, and others will follow the three-layer symptom/diagnosis/treatment plan path.

■ *Successes/wins:* This supplemental section of the primary LDM board (we will talk about a different type of LDM board in the following paragraphs) is that of successes and wins. It is critical to have a section for these on the LDM board! It helps the team remember that the LDM board is resulting in positive improvements and change. Also, organizations (and hospitals in particular) are very good at focusing on what is going wrong, but find it difficult to remember what is going right and what is working well. Also, when doing LDM board tours or using LDM boards as "model lines" to inspire and demonstrate to others, the teams see the WIIFM and positive change from the successes and wins on the LDM boards.

■ *Operational/prioritization boards (higher level boards):* The final section of the LDM board that we will explore is either a part of the main LDM board, or commonly a stand-alone supplementary LDM board. The primary focus of this board is different, but not mutually exclusive of the "problem-solving" LDM board. The problem that this supplementary "operational/prioritization" board addresses is that managers and teams that work on projects or multiple initiatives have multitudes of competing priorities and tasks that can easily overwhelm a team, and in this sort of situation, certain fundamental dysfunctions materialize that can be addressed through the proper use of the operation/prioritization LDM board.

When teams have numerous actions and initiatives that involve competing priorities, these action items usually fall along a wide spectrum of difficulty and impact or importance and urgency. (These are the two most common axes for these prioritization boards.) For this section, we will explore the importance and urgency continuum, as this is the most readily applicable set of characteristics that are useful to the teams.

Using the axes of urgency and importance (represented as a $2 \times 2 = 4$ quadrant axis) to view these multitudes of competing priorities and tasks, we will conceptually explore the natural dysfunctions that commonly occur without a disciplined system.

■ *High urgency/high importance (first priority):* Teams naturally focus on high urgency/high importance items, so these tasks aren't usually the biggest problem, unless they don't realize that they fall into this quadrant without a disciplined and visual system such as this. A problem that can occur is that groups sometimes tend to want to put everything in this quadrant, which becomes a problem because it defeats the entire point of prioritizing work if everything is urgent and important! This problem is actually a great flag for a problem when using this framework. It is an indicator that the team needs to look at and triage the work more critically than they did before, or they may need leadership support to help prioritize these items.

■ *Low urgency/high importance (second priority):* The next two quadrants are where the true value of the prioritization comes into play! As we mentioned, the high urgency/high importance quadrant is a natural focus of efforts for most teams. But after that quadrant, the human mind can begin to lead us astray! It becomes a struggle between low urgency/high importance and high urgency/low importance. Therefore, it is a competition between the "high" aspects of each of these: importance versus urgency. Which do you think you would choose? The natural instinct is to react to a looming deadline or something that has to happen right away, whether it is important or not. In an operational environment like a hospital, there is no shortage of high-urgency tasks, so the average manager and team tend to "live" in the high urgency quadrant, of either high or low importance. Therefore, "urgency" tends to trump "importance," which is the wrong way to manage a project! While some urgent items need to be addressed, there must be discipline to focus on the high importance/low urgency items. If we don't, we end up playing "defense" as low urgency turns into high urgency when we procrastinate and deprioritize something long enough (It is the same way in life, isn't it?). Therefore, this matrix emphasizes that importance comes first, and urgency comes second, which is why this quadrant is the second priority.

■ *High urgency/low importance (third priority):* As we discussed in the previous paragraph, importance trumps urgency, and now that we are down to the two low importance quadrants, it is a choice between high and low urgency. Given these choices, high urgency trumps low urgency, so this quadrant is the third priority.

■ *Low urgency/low importance (fourth priority):* Low urgency/low importance items, just like high urgency/high importance items, don't tend to be the primary issue, as this is generally work that we only get to when all of the other quadrants in the matrix have been addressed. Therefore, these are listed as the fourth priority (see Figure 3.10).

In summary, this prioritization board is a critical (and simple!) visual tool to help teams effectively manage and prioritize the multitude of tasks that often overwhelm teams who need to implement a large and multifaceted

Figure 3.10   LDM board "priority matrix."

project (such as a VSM project or any other large project in a hospital). The human mind (and a team is a collection of human minds!) defaults to prioritizing urgency over importance, when importance should generally trump urgency. By forcing teams to "sort" activities into these different quadrants, and engaging leaders well in this, it leads to more effective and efficient project management and leadership engagement.

Journal

Use this page to reflect on your LDM board progress thus far. What are the portions of the LDM boards that leaders and staff are struggling with? Why?

Reference

Rosenthal, R. 1966. *Experimenter Effects in Behavioral Research.* New York: Appleton-Century-Crofts, p. 464.

Chapter 4

Leadership Rounds

Much like a physician rounds with a patient to learn, understand, and ascertain progress toward the treatment plan and the patient's diagnosis (DX) (learning what's working and what needs to be adjusted based on that particular patient's response and progress), leaders must regularly round with their middle managers and front-line units to ensure staff understand their goals and are tracking and managing their Lean daily management system (LDM) boards (coaching and developing staff to keep up with their symptoms, DX, and treatment plans on key LDM board goals). Additionally, leaders need to be looking for ideas/actions that staff may be struggling with and escalating them to the senior leadership level for prioritization, resourcing, and support.

Age wrinkles the body. Quitting wrinkles the soul.

–Douglas MacArthur

Leadership rounds are the "glue" that holds the LDM system together. Problem-solving LDM boards alone will focus front-line units on key goals and get them "diagnosing" and "treating" the "symptoms" on their LDM board; however, at some point they will run into problems that are too big, too complicated or too politically sensitive for them to solve on their own. The leadership round ensures these problems are getting escalated and addressed daily. Also, the leader rounds are a key cultural indicator of the importance (or lack thereof!) of LDM to the organization (which is represented through leaders). If the leaders are rounding and engaged, supportive, and following through on their rounds, it tells the teams that LDM is important to their leaders (and therefore the organization as a whole), which is a tremendous motivator! This was notably demonstrated through the Hawthorne effect, where the mere act of observing workers and groups motivated them to improve and work harder.

Senior leadership must be the first to develop their LDM board and round. Senior leaders cannot delegate rounding and LDM board development and management to middle management and front-line units. If the senior leaders take a "wait and see" attitude to LDM, it will quickly "die on the vine" as middle management and front-line staff will quickly (and accurately) ascertain that this isn't important to the organization (because of the lack of senior leadership engagement and involvement). The principle of "leading from the front" is of utmost importance here, as the visible engagement and involvement of the senior leadership sends a strong message to the entire organization.

> *We are not retreating—we are advancing in another direction.*
>
> **–Douglas MacArthur**

Leadership rounds are uniquely different than simply "management by walking around." Leadership rounds fundamentally are reinforcing the LDM system by doing the following things (see the three rounding conversations on page 22):

- Senior leaders ensure middle managers are tracking and progressing with their LDM boards. Middle management LDM boards' goals and measures should align with senior leadership LDM boards over time— initially the LDM boards may focus on problems that are more relevant and important to that particular middle manager and their department to get them engaged in the process, but eventually the middle management LDM board should reflect those key departmental goals that align with higher level organizational and senior leadership LDM board's goals and measures.
- Leaders ensure that actions/ideas that front-line units are struggling with are escalating to the middle management LDM board and either being addressed or being escalated up to the senior leadership level.

LDM Tip: The goal is for roughly 80% of the problems to be resolved between the front-line unit LDM boards and the middle management LDM boards and leader rounds—the remaining 20% of the toughest ideas/actions and problems escalate to the senior leadership LDM board for prioritization and resourcing.

■ Leaders ensure that middle managers and front-line units are managing their LDM boards. Leaders ensure that their staff are tracking their goals/symptoms daily, analyzing/problem-solving/diagnosing key gaps on those goals daily, and identifying ideas/actions/treatment plans daily to address those key gaps from their analysis/DX. Essentially leaders are driving small, focused plan–do–study–acts (PDSAs) daily with their staff around the LDM board.

LDM Tip: Let staff pull Lean tools from you as they learn how to problem solve. For example, try not to push an A3 problem-solving form on them until they are ready for it. How will you know? They will be stuck on a problem and need the A3 problem-solving form to help them "see" the problem more clearly.

■ Leaders coach middle managers to develop their front-line units to problem solve on their key LDM board goals in the "Gemba" or "where the work happens."
■ Leaders ensure that middle management and front-line supervisors are following and executing the LDM system each day (conducting leadership rounds daily, escalating ideas as needed, supporting problem solving with their front-line units, etc.)
■ Leaders establish a daily "cadence" for improvement/progress toward front-line unit, middle management, and organizational goals. Leadership rounds drive the shift from monthly/weekly LDM board tracking, management, and progress to daily LDM board tracking, management, and progress. Leadership rounds create a culture of execution and "getting things done" today.
■ Leaders encourage and celebrate LDM board problem solving (coaching middle managers and front-line staff to solve problems by visually using their LDM board so leaders and support groups can quickly understand and learn what's working, what didn't work and why, and what they can do to help).

Rounding Using the "Socratic Method"

The Socratic method is a form of inquiry and discussion between individuals, based on asking and answering questions to stimulate critical thinking and to illuminate ideas.

> *I know that I am intelligent, because I know that I know nothing.*
>
> **–Socrates**

This approach is critical to learning and is the basis for Lean leadership. This includes leadership rounds, LDM board problem solving, strategy deployment (Hoshin planning), and leader daily discipline planning.

> *Nature has given us two ears, two eyes and but one tongue—to the end that we should hear and see more than we speak.*
>
> **–Socrates**

Leader Round Example

So let's walk through a leadership round (An example of an early rounding session to demonstrate some of the challenges you will encounter in the beginning. We will go through an additional leader-round in a more mature state later.):

Senior leader (Jane) first looks to her leader daily discipline plan to see which middle manager and front-line LDM board units she will round with today (leader round schedule as per the leader daily discipline plan).

Jane brings her leader round notebook (leader round notebook is recommended to document findings and follow-up actions from the round). This leader-round notebook should be brought to every leader round to help keep a running journal on progress, follow-up, and so on.

Jane first rounds with her middle manager (John) and his respective LDM board (departmental round).

Senior leader (Jane) opens: Good morning John, I am here for our scheduled leadership round with you and a couple of key front-line units.

Middle manager (John): Hi Jane, we have been swamped with several staff out so I will try to give you the best information I can.

Senior leader (Jane): John, I completely appreciate the challenges you and your team face daily which is why these leadership rounds are so important to me and for your staff. I need to make sure that those key problems that staff need help with are being addressed daily; also the round gives me a chance to learn more about these problems so I can escalate these problems your staff may be stuck on to the senior leadership level. Finally it gives me a chance to help you and your staff gain clarity on what's most important today—helping them prioritize the most important ideas/actions to be working on and problem solving on today.

Middle manager (John): Wow, that's great Jane; we really need the help down here on the floor.

Senior leader (Jane): So John, what are the key departmental goals you are tracking on your LDM board?

Middle manager (John): Jane, we are tracking provider schedule utilization, no-shows, patient satisfaction, wait times, and quality, but the problem is that I simply don't have the time to collect the data and track each of these every day; it's a lot of work and I have so many fires I have to put out constantly throughout the day.

Senior leader (Jane): John, I completely understand how busy you are; so let's try to pick one goal/measure to start with first. I am more concerned with you and your staff understanding the LDM board/ leader round (LDM) process first before we try to track and manage all of our key metrics together. So organizationally we are really focused on our quality scores and getting those up; however, which one of these goals is most important to you and your staff right now?

Middle manager (John): The biggest frustration for our staff and providers right now is with the electronic medical record (EMR) system and the number of kick-outs, delays, and overall sluggishness of the system. If we could get help with that it would really help get staff and providers on board with our LDM boards and LDM system.

LDM Tip: Jane uses this real problem presented by John to get him to use the LDM board to measure/track, manage, problem solve, and escalate ideas. Remember, create a pull for LDM where you can versus a push!

Senior leader (Jane): John, what can we track with respect to the EMR on our LDM board that would show progress and get us problem solving around that issue?

Middle manager (John): That's a tough one ... staff generally refers to the number of times the EMR kicks them out per day ... maybe we can track that?

Senior leader (Jane): I think that's a good start ... let's build an LDM board tracking the number of EMR kick-outs per day on the *y*-axis and day of the week on the *x*-axis. At first we will just track the number of kick-outs just to get a sense of what a good goal may be. As we track this goal daily, let's identify the "whys" on the DX part of our LDM board (identifying different whys and how many times those whys happen over a week or two ... using a histogram). I will help you set up the LDM board and send you a histogram template for your staff to start using. Let's track the number of kick-outs per day and the reasons why (histogram) this week and I will conduct another round next week at the same time to see what the data looks like. We can ask staff what they think the key "whys" are from the histogram and what some ideas/actions we can try that day to address the kick-outs ... does that sound reasonable?

LDM Tip: You may want to bring your Lean coach/LDM Sensei along for your first few rounds!

Middle manager (John): Absolutely Jane ... I can see how my staff unit LDM boards, focusing on this one key goal (reducing the number of EMR kick-outs) daily and annotating the key reasons why they had kick-outs on those heavy days on the histogram, will start to get them thinking more critically and deeply about this problem. I can build the new symptom chart for this one as you recommended.

Senior leader (Jane): Great John ... I will send the histogram template to you for your board and your staff's LDM boards and be back next week to conduct a leadership round.

LDM Tip: Take it slow at first! Take baby steps to tracking managing and improving performance. Get them tracking "EMR kick-outs" first, writing down their "DX" or whys, and details around the kick-outs per day and finally get them to think about one idea they can try today or this week, then come back next week and check progress.

Leader rounds can be flexible to the culture of your organization; however, certain aspects of leadership rounds need to be consistent.

Step 1: Use the Socratic method when you round with middle managers and front-line staff. As Socrates reminds us "Use both of your eyes, both your ears and a single tongue" in that ratio. Starting with the symptoms, let staff explain how they are doing. Listen to the responses. Ask yourself: "Do they truly understand their goals or are they just going through the motions?" Listen to the level of detail that staff gives you. If they missed a goal on a specific day, did they annotate why on their "DX" section of the board? Is there an idea or action that addresses that particular "why"? If not, dive in and ask staff what ideas they believe could close the gap? Are there "whys" that need more detail?

Step 2: Ask staff what they believe the key "whys" to be and then make sure they document that on their "DX" section of their LDM board.

Ask the staff if they notice any trends from one day to the next on their board, and get them to see the board as a tool to help them "see" opportunities. For example, "I noticed that every Monday we have the greatest no-shows, why is that? What could we do to improve that?"

Step 3: Look at the action plan (treatment plan) and look for updates, details, action owners, due dates, and the need for help/escalation if it's been sitting there too long.

If you are rounding with a middle manager, ask the middle manager if they need help with any ideas that are escalated, but try to allow problem solving to occur before you simply pull it in as your escalated idea/action.

When rounding, it is often helpful to round by service line to pull in problems across that particular service line or process.

Leader grand round (LGR) is a great way to establish rounding by service line or process. Senior leaders identify key service lines or processes within the hospital and round daily on those units and LDM boards within that process. Leader daily discipline is designed to round by service line. Various hospital floor units within a process are prepared for senior leadership to round daily, review LDM board symptoms, DX, and treatment plans and escalate ideas/actions that aren't getting traction or need senior leadership support. LGR typically happens at a set time in the morning and a "no meeting" time is established to allow staff and leaders to get through the rounds (typically 1 hour for the entire grand round from back of the process to the front).

Leader grand rounds should start at the back of the process and work their way forward. Rounding this way ensures that as the leader rounds closer to the front of the process, problems and bottlenecks that are piling up at the end of the process can be communicated and shared with staff and their LDM boards at the front of the process. Over time, leader grand rounds on key service lines will create alignment of key LDM boards and start to get staff thinking and problem solving in a more service line/process-centered way. This will create a "pull" for value stream mapping project teams to highlight waste and bottlenecks across the service line/value streams.

Leader grand rounds is one of the first real steps to creating a service line/process-centered organization, because it starts to connect those units in a service line/process in a very natural way through leader grand rounds and alignment over time of their LDM boards. Early on as leaders conduct grand rounds, the units will tend to focus on problems and issues that lie within their functional area which makes sense, and as leader grand rounds mature, units start to learn more about problems and issues upstream and downstream. Front-line units start to understand (from the leader grand rounds process) what specific challenges they are creating for the upstream and downstream units and bigger ideas that span the service line/process start to surface.

LDM boards across the service line/process will start to incorporate goals that measure how well they are supporting their upstream and downstream units; once again the organization starts moving naturally toward process versus functional thinking and problem solving.

The simple act of leader grand rounds establishes the importance of the service line/process. Once leaders and staff start thinking and problem solving around process, significant opportunities start to surface that silo'd functional thinking and problem solving simply can't uncover. The biggest gaps or waste in any process are typically those steps or touch-points between departments or functional areas that make up a process.

In the clinic setting, it may be easier to round by pods or as groups of pods (specialists, family practice, etc.)

Vertical/Departmental Rounding Rules

- Middle managers round daily with at least—two to three front-line unit/pod LDM boards.
- Senior leaders round at least weekly with one middle manager LDM board and two to three front-line LDM boards (daily if possible).
- Follow up on escalated ideas weekly.

Rounding Do's and Don'ts

- **Do:** Celebrate small successes on LDM board development, such as simply getting the board up and plotting performance consistently daily.
- **Don't:** Underestimate how much of a big shift or change this new habit is for staff; it will be scary for them at first and they don't want to look bad!
- **Do:** Celebrate successful tracking and management of LDM boards even if they are not hitting their goal yet. Remember, they are new to this LDM process and will need to develop their "LDM muscles"!
- **Do:** Celebrate valiant "failures" where you can. Celebrate any idea that didn't move the dial, but the team learned from. If it was worth trying and didn't succeed or work out, it was a "successful failure"!
- **Do:** Celebrate "symptoms" that hit goal consistently—challenge the team to go even further or find a new measure they may need to work on and up on the LDM board. If the team has consistently hit the goal for quite some time, you might be able to move the measure from the main LDM board (driver measure) to a location off the main LDM board (watcher measure).

LDM Exposes Leadership Gaps

LDM boards can be used as a gauge for unit leadership and talent. For example, if you notice that a particular unit doesn't seem to "get it" because they aren't plotting or updating their LDM boards or capturing their "whys" on the DX portion of their board or actively coming up with, and implementing, ideas/actions (treatment plan) to close the gaps on their goals, your initial instincts may be to think that it's a form of passive resistance. Don't assume anything until you have had time to better understand the unit supervisor and the team!

There may be a fundamental disconnect in the measures and goals they are tracking and what "they" believe are the "real" problems. Try to get what the "unit" believes are the issues and start tracking those first! The key is to get the unit and leader to learn, understand and use LDM first, and then point the boards in the right direction of key organizational goals.

For Example

Jane: Hi John, I am here for our follow-up scheduled 9 AM leader-round with you and two front-line units.

John: Sounds great Jane, let's go visit Joanne's pod (team lead).

Jane arrives with John at Joanne's pod:

Jane: Hi Joanne, please tell me about your symptoms (key board goals)?

Joanne: Jane, we have been tied up with EMR kick-outs and slowness issues (clue!) and haven't been able to keep up with the board.

Jane: OK, Joanne, you know this board really helps me understand where I need to help you guys and when you don't track and manage it, it's a lot harder for me to help you and your unit … what if we tracked EMR kick-outs and issues which seems to be the real issue with your unit right now?

Joanne: That would really be helpful, Jane! We have seen a big rise in EMR issues in our pod, which takes more time and throws off our schedule quite a bit and we all get so far behind.

Jane: What if we measured the number of EMR kick-outs and issues per day on your LDM board to help us understand with greater detail what and when these EMR issues occur?

Joanne: I believe it would help, Jane.

Jane: Let's set up the new symptom (goal) on your LDM board now. What if we measured days of the week on the *x*-axis and number of EMR issues per day on the *y*-axis, then track how many times EMR issues we have each day through this week, starting tomorrow? Be sure to document the reasons "why" you don't hit goal that day so you don't lose that information or forget … we want to be as specific as possible on the "whys." A good way to get started is to list your top five whys and then simply put an X by the whys you believe affected your missing goal that day. Finally, as you start to see which whys have the most occurrences (Tip: Try using a blank histogram with the top five reasons filled out so the team just has to place an X by the reasons each day throughout the week) and are the easiest to improve upon, start identifying ideas and actions with owners and follow-up dates (on your treatment plan) that will address your key "whys" and reasons.

LDM Tip: The LDM board reads like a complete PDSA cycle from the symptom to the DX to the treatment plan; it gets the team into the basic PDSA cycle which eventually leads them to use foundational Lean tools and methods such as A3s, 5S, standard work, etc.).

Jane: I will be back in 1 week to see how you are doing.

Jane writes down a follow-up date on her leader daily discipline notebook. Jane then pulls John aside and discusses what just occurred.

Jane: John, what are your thoughts about our round today? (Socratic method)

John: Jane, my sincerest apologies, I pulled Joanne into my office beforehand as we discussed last week and explained to her about building our LDM board focusing on EMR kick-outs, and actually gave her an example and the histogram you sent me for the DX section, but apparently she hasn't been able to get it going … I should have followed up (rounded) with her to ensure she was getting the support she needed to get the LDM board started.

Jane: John, thanks for that honest answer. Let's make sure you reach out to me if they get stuck on any part of the LDM board before my next round, so I can help sooner OK?

John: Absolutely . . . . We will be ready next time!

1 Week Later

Jane arrives at John's office.

Jane: Hi, John, I am here for our follow-up round with Joanne's pod (as per Jane's leader daily discipline plan).

John: Great, Joanne's been expecting you.

Jane: John, this time I'd like you to conduct the leader round with Joanne if you feel comfortable with that.

John: Well … I don't know if I am ready for that just yet.

Jane: John, I will tell you what, why don't you watch me conduct this round and then on our next round I'd like you to start conducting them?

John: OK.

Jane and John walk down to Joanne's pod.

Jane: Hi, Joanne, I'm here to follow up on our LDM board EMR issues. Can you tell me how this past week went (use your key leader round conversation-scripting here to guide you)?

Joanne: Well … it went really good Jane, no problems at all!

Jane: Thanks, Joanne, but can you show me on your LDM board how many issues you had per day and any "whys" and ideas/actions that your pod may have come up with since our last round?

Joanne: Well … we didn't get a chance to track every day but we've put in plenty of work-tickets for IT and feel good that the EMR issues should be resolved! (Tip: This is an attempt to placate the leader, while passively resisting the need to track and manage their key LDM board metrics.)

Jane: (Coaching moment) Joanne, it's really important to track our EMR issues daily so we can learn what issues happen on what days; there's a lot of good detailed specific information that come from this process that will then help IT (if indeed we need IT) better support us. Let's start tracking the number of EMR issues per day and just that for now. I will come back next week with John and we will go through your LDM board to include the symptoms (tracking the number of EMR issues per day), the "whys" (DX) and ideas/actions to solve for those key "whys" (treatment plan) … is that doable?

Joanne: Absolutely … I think we just got a little confused.

Jane: I completely understand Joanne, it's a learning process…. . I'll see you in a week.

Jane and John walk back up to John's office.

Jane: So, John, what are your thoughts about that leader round?

John: Well, we obviously still weren't completely prepared and it sounds like Joanne was a little confused.

Jane: John, what could we have done differently?

John: Well, I probably should have checked her board a couple of times before your round to make sure she was progressing. OK?

Jane: I understand how busy you are John, but these boards are truly the way that I know how to help Joanne and you … whatever is on that board gets my attention and priority.

John: Got it.

Jane: So next week I would like you to round and I will listen/support you. I'd like for you to round with Joanne once per day to make sure she is tracking her EMR issues and getting daily reinforcement.

John: Will do.

1 Week Later

Jane arrives at John's office.

Jane: John, I am here for my follow-up round with Joanne.

John: Great we are ready this time and excited to share our progress.

Jane: Are you ready to lead the round?

John: Absolutely, I've been rounding every day with Joanne and we went beyond tracking our EMR issues, we captured key whys and ideas/actions.

Jane: Great, let's go, see!

Jane and John arrive at Joanne's pod LDM board.

John: Hi, Joanne, we are here to round on our EMR issues on our LDM board.

Joanne: Great! … Monday started off horribly as usual with 15 EMR issues … key whys from that day were 10 kick-outs and 5 slow running occurrences. Tuesday was better at eight EMR issues, six kick-outs and two slow occurrences—Wednesday at five EMR issues, three kick-outs and two slow occurrences; Thursday up a little at eight EMR issues, five kick-outs, and three slow occurrences; and Friday we had zero issues (slower day). We all realized that the beginning of the week was the worst and as we moved through the week the EMR issues got a little better (except Thursday).

John: So, what ideas did you come up with?

Joanne: Well, one idea was to have IT shadow us on Monday, our toughest day. We have already scheduled for Arnie (IT) to come out Monday and shadow us.

Jane: Great! Is there anything I can help you with so far?

Joanne: Not right now, Jane. We've got our action plan for Arnie and are excited for him to shadow us on Mondays and get to the bottom of some of these kick-outs!

John and Jane leave.

This gives you a sense for the leader round dialogue and follow-up necessary to "engage" a middle manager and front-line staff. It's not an overnight process and you will need to expect passive resistance; however, use the Socratic method to coach, guide, and develop your staff.

Journal

At this point you have created some key LDM boards across your organization and started leadership rounds to reinforce tracking, management, and progress on these boards. Reflect on what's working and what may not be working so well in the following. Are certain leaders passively resisting? Why? Are senior leaders rounding or are they expecting you to round for them?

Chapter 5

Leader Daily Discipline

Leader daily discipline is often the last component of the lean daily management (LDM) system to get implemented. Leader daily discipline defines HOW and WHEN the leader will develop and maintain the LDM system. What days, times, and routes will you round with your middle manager boards and unit boards? Will you create a rounding schedule that follows along key service lines?

When will you follow through on escalated ideas from your units? When will you coach your staff on problem solving? When will you recognize their successes? Leader daily discipline forces the leader to build a plan (daily, weekly, monthly) and schedule for all to see (peers, staff, and boss) identifying those key LDM activities you will be following up with on a daily, weekly, and monthly basis. The intent isn't to lock the leader into a rigid routine, but more to set an expectation that key LDM activities need daily, weekly, and monthly attention. This sets a "cadence" in place for the organization to measure and track key goals, analyze gaps (diagnosis) and understand key root causes and identify ideas and actions (treatment plan) to address the key gaps. Key whys and root causes and escalated key ideas staff are "stuck" on are addressed daily.

Leader daily discipline's "cadence" also ensures that leadership follows through on key escalated ideas/actions as well as ongoing coaching (in the Gemba) of middle managers and staff on LDM board management and problem solving. Some escalated ideas will turn into more formal A3s or Kaizen events, others will simply need resourcing and support from other departmental leaders.

Without leader daily discipline, leaders are left to try and "work-in" LDM building activities (leader rounds, LDM board coaching, escalated idea follow-through, etc.) as they can within their already overbooked schedule.

Leaders often resist leader daily discipline because they believe it "locks" them into a "rigid" schedule; however, LDM actually gives everyone (senior leader, middle manager, and staff) something to anchor to in a world of daily firefighting and shifting priorities.

Leader daily discipline clarifies what activities are most important on a daily, weekly, monthly basis within your department. Without some sort of regular cadence the leader and staff are overwhelmed by the chaos of everyday operations and firefighting and progress toward key goals takes a backseat to "keeping afloat." LDM activities like LDM board management, leadership rounds, updating daily LDM boards, analyzing gaps, identifying ideas and actions, and follow-through on escalated actions either don't happen or happen inconsistently.

Staff and managers often state that they are too "shorthanded" to track and manage an LDM board and participate in regular leader rounds because they only know the day-to day-firefighting that has become their way of life. Once staff engages in one key goal and metric to start and progress is made toward that goal, LDM and their "board" becomes the focal point for progress, problems, ideas and staff learns that "what goes on that board gets attention, support and gets better."

Leader daily discipline clarifies accountability for leader and staff alike. Leaders resist at first; however, over time leaders realize leaders daily discipline creates a rhythm, cadence, and flow of management and leadership that was missing before.

Leader daily discipline allows leaders across multiple sites to become more aligned in "how" they lead and manage. Successful leaders will share their leader daily discipline with those that struggle. Leader daily discipline is also a great learning tool for new leaders coming into the department or the greater organization to quickly understand "how" the department or greater organization gets things done or "executes."

Leader daily discipline also becomes a more uniform way to measure leadership and management development and progress across the leadership ranks. Leaders that struggle to follow their own leader daily discipline will not have the discipline to develop their staff to manage their LDM boards and drive progress on their key goals.

Leader daily discipline is most effective when the chief executive officer (CEO) and chief operating officer set the example by creating their own leader daily discipline and then executing to their new plan.

Leaders should work with their staff to identify the best days and times to conduct leadership rounds, daily LDM board management, and follow up on escalated ideas. Leaders should also share their leader daily discipline with peers, their boss, and staff to ensure alignment, clarity, and priorities.

LDM tip: Start small with your leader daily discipline, begin with one unit, one middle manager and plan/schedule leadership rounds, LDM board setup and development, escalated action follow-up— try this for a couple of weeks, make improvements, once this unit and managers are effectively practicing LDM, update your leader daily discipline and deploy three to four more units and middle managers, make adjustment again, further deploy until your entire department is integrated into your leader daily discipline. Finally share your new leader daily discipline with support groups (information technology, etc.) and your boss to integrate them into your new LDM schedule/plan (leader daily discipline); see example shown in Figure 5.1.

Leader standard work day

Monday		Tuesday	Wednesday	Thursday	Friday
7:50am	CK e-mail/VM	CK e-mail/VM	CK e-mail/VM	CK e-mail/VM	CK e-mail/VM
8:30am	IP Rounding	IP Rounding	IP Rounding	IP Rounding	IP Rounding
9:00am	Charges/Pyramis	Charges/Pyramis	Charges/Pyramis	Charges/Pyramis	Charges/Pyramis
10:30am	Desk work	Desk work	Desk work	Desk work	Desk work
12:30am	Ordering	Staff rounding	ABG check in	Monthly list	PTO Request
1:00pm	QA/QI	QA/QI	QA/QI	QA/QI	QA/QI
2:00pm	Follow up/Huddle	Follow up/Huddle	Follow up/Huddle	Follow up/Huddle	Follow up/Huddle
3:00pm	OP Rounding	OP Rounding	OP Rounding	OP Rounding	OP Rounding
4:00pm	Close day/Purge	Close day/Purge	Close day/Purge	Close day/Purge	Close day/Purge
(Desk work: kronos, policies, high 5s bills)					

Monthly list: one up, finalize QA/QI, ventilator days, med dir sheets, eval follow-up, schedule, rounding w/dr, stop light
ABG check in: Peer review, maintenance, ext qc, qc data list/levy, api, competency

Figure 5.1 Leader daily discipline example.

Once your CEO has his or her leader daily discipline started use that as a starting point for your C-level leaders. Set aside time with each senior leader to develop their baseline leader daily discipline. For example,

Lean coach (Jerry): Good morning, Dr. Fleming, I will be supporting you and your team with their goals. To get us into a "daily" cadence or rhythm for tracking, measuring, and managing our LDM boards, we will need to develop leader daily discipline.

Chief medical officer (CMO) (Dr. Fleming): Jerry, I really appreciate your help. I have a very busy schedule, but will do what I can to support you and the team to achieve our goals. Approximately how much time will it take for me to "round" and support our LDM boards?

Lean coach (Jerry): I'd like to start small and deploy LDM boards and leadership rounds at a pace that works best for you and your staff. We can start with just one key area and round with them once per day for 15–20 minutes to get an understanding of the rounding process and give the unit time to mature and grow/learn their LDM boards and get some traction. Once we feel comfortable with that one board and our supporting round, we can revisit our leader daily discipline to think about other areas to add in.

CMO (Dr. Fleming): That sounds great, Jerry, but how much time will that take over the long haul?

Jerry: Over time each of your key units will have an LDM board and will need supporting rounds. I will be working with your medical directors to ensure they round with their respective areas. We will focus our rounds only on those areas that need the greatest help (typically one leader round per day with those areas that need the most help that day). We can flex that as your schedule needs; however, I recommend we build these rounds into your leader daily discipline and place them on your calendar. To start we will conduct one leader round for 15–20 minutes per day (let's block 30 minutes initially to give us plenty of time).

CMO (Dr. Fleming): That sounds reasonable, Jerry. Can you set those meetings up for me in my calendar and send me our updated leader daily discipline?

Lean Coach (Jerry): Absolutely, Dr. Fleming. I'll get you a copy of your leader daily discipline and set up our daily leader rounds on your calendar with your assistant. I'd like to post your leader daily discipline on all of the LDM boards in your area as they go up, so everyone knows when you will round with them and what is expected.

LDM tip: What prevents most leaders from doing process improvement? It's not on their calendars! Therefore leaders don't get around to those process improvement activities to sustain those improvement ideas from their staff and follow up. Leader daily discipline forces the leader to put process improvement activities on their calendar and thereby prioritize it.

When first building leader daily discipline with your senior leaders it may be easier to get all of them to build collective leader daily discipline together during a time that is already used by all senior leaders for something else.

For example, if you are already managing LDM boards with your senior leaders daily, pick a day of the week that all leaders agree to set aside for senior leadership rounds together or for leadership grand rounds. Leadership grand rounds around a key service line or process and the daily senior leadership LDM board review become the first two LDM activities on each senior leader's "leader daily discipline."

Leaders oftentimes will learn better together in a safe environment where they can watch others first. Ultimately the goal is to get senior leaders to round effectively individually with their respective areas, but in the interim it may be helpful to have a combined grand round to get everyone understanding leadership rounds and on board.

As you develop leader grand rounds use your senior leader LDM board to guide where the senior leadership team rounds. Let the senior leadership team drive which areas to round with each week based on their senior leadership LDM board metrics and gaps. If you've already established leader grand rounds around service lines, use the senior leader LDM board to drive what the leaders look for as they round. For example, if patient satisfaction is taking a hit on the senior leader LDM board, look for evidence of declining patient satisfaction on the unit level LDM boards and what their diagnosis and treatment plans are. If patient satisfaction isn't being tracked and measured, that's an action in itself!

Prepare the senior leadership team to use the "Socratic" method (see Chapter 4). Senior leaders will need close coaching and support early on.

Help each senior leader prepare ahead of time for grand rounds by developing a grand rounds notebook for them.

Some organizations have grand rounds set up by key service lines or processes to ensure these key services or processes get the support they need daily. An example of a service line is the operating room (OR) service line or process. A grand round for this service line would start with the Med-surge LDM board, then move to an intensive care unit (ICU) board, postanesthesia care unit (PACU) board, OR board, Pre-Op board, sterile processing board, and finish up with the admissions board (for the OR). Leadership would round with each board, learn and understand the key gaps (symptoms), analysis, (diagnosis) and ideas/actions (treatment plan) for each area within the service line. Leadership would pull escalated ideas/actions as well as ensure all boards are aligned with their senior leadership LDM board. Leadership would also ensure that key gaps in performance from the senior leaders' LDM board are prioritized with these lower level boards. Finally leadership is helping to "connect" each of the OR boards and staff by sharing successes and challenges across the service line (bird's eye view of the gaps, analysis, and successful ideas).

The benefits of consistent grand rounds by service line or department is that staff begin to expect and look forward to senior leadership support, coaching, escalation, and problem solving on the floor during those days. The organization, over time develops a "cadence" and culture of daily improvement.

Leader daily discipline documents what leaders are doing with respect to developing and managing their LDM system. Every senior leader should audit/review the leader daily discipline of their leaders to ensure there is alignment up and down the chain of command. The senior leaders' daily discipline typically drives that of their staff. For example, all leaders may be rounding on patient satisfaction on Tuesdays from the senior leadership's LDM board to director's LDM boards all the way down to front-line staffs' LDM boards. There's an alignment and focus that happens on Tuesdays around patient satisfaction that never occurred before and it includes rounding, review of LDM boards, escalation of ideas/actions staff is stuck on, resourcing of those escalated ideas/actions and coaching and support along the way. Leader daily discipline, designed thoughtfully and effectively, will begin to change your culture round by round, day by day to a culture of execution and daily problem solving. There are very few surprises for leadership on what the real issues on the floor are. There are very few surprises for staff on what is expected from senior leadership. Goals become clearer and understood on levels like never before (see Figure 5.2).

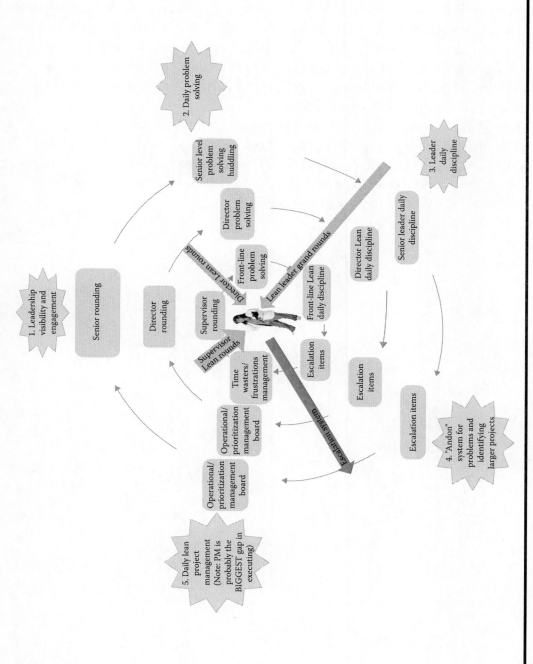

Figure 5.2 Detailed working Lean daily management model.

Journal

By now your LDM program is well underway! You have LDM boards up and running in many areas of the hospital. Leadership is learning how to round effectively. Leader daily discipline "schedules" are starting to show up on LDM boards; so staff and leaders know when rounds will occur and when follow-up on escalated ideas will occur. Staff is beginning to believe that leadership is committed to this change!

Take this time to reflect what you've accomplished. How many LDM boards do you have in place? What progress have staff and leaders made toward their LDM board goals thus far? Have you celebrated those successes yet? Is there a leader and front-line board you feel could be a "model" for LDM? How can they help you develop others?

Chapter 6

Linking Lean Daily Management to Strategy Deployment (Hoshin Planning)

After discussing and setting up the infrastructure for the Lean daily management (LDM) system (LDM boards, leader rounding, leader daily discipline, Lean projects), it is critical to take one step back and ask yourself "why are we doing this?" Part of the answer to this question is that we are trying to solve problems, eliminate waste, develop our people, improve flow, and add value to the customer. If we take one more step back and look at an even higher perspective, we are trying to strengthen our overall organization and develop a system that will help us dynamically and effectively achieve our organization's goals, provide long-term stable employment for the individuals and teams we are employing, and provide value to our patients and the community and society as a whole.

If we focus exclusively on solving problems, eliminating waste, and improving flow without an overall objective or guiding vision, then we are in danger of "popcorn Kaizen" and improving efficiencies without necessarily linking these improvements to the "bottom line" or creating a unified patient experience or overall organization vision. This could also be looked at as the difference between "tactics" and "strategy" without linking all of the "tactics" together to move toward the "strategy," then we are in danger of "winning the battles but losing the war."

Fortunately, the Lean tool kit has a powerful, effective, and disciplined way of achieving this, but it requires persistence and diligence to be successful. When linked with LDM, these two approaches (LDM and Hoshin planning) are mutually supportive and beneficial, which will be explained further in the following sections. The critical concept to understand is that the strategy and vision of the organization needs to be linked from the top level of the organization down to the front lines, with detailed and thoughtful translation and buy-in at all levels.

When this is done properly, these translated and negotiated goals and objectives can easily be transferred to the structure and function of the LDM boards that have been previously explored. The LDM boards then become the "how" to much of the "what" that was identified through the Hoshin planning, and they become a tangible and visible way for leaders at all levels to physically and visually assess the strength of the linkages and progress of the teams toward these goals. This is an example of LDM boards being used effectively to assess the strength and continuity of strategy deployment in an organization (where are we making progress, where are we not, and where do we have or don't have LDM boards?).

Hoshin planning is, at its most basic level, cascaded, negotiated, translated, and quantified goals that begin at the top of the organization (mission/vision/values/strategy/goals) through to the front lines. When done properly, there is "line of sight" for all members of an organization that provide relevance and meaning for their improvement efforts and daily tasks. If done properly, anyone can explain how focusing on improving a specific activity or task contributes to the overall organization's goals or objectives. An example of this from a historical perspective was when President Kennedy visited Cape Canaveral and asked a janitor what his job was; he responded that "he was helping to put a man on the moon!" A parallel example for healthcare would be to ask the same question of a housekeeper working in the operating room (OR) and instead of them saying that "they cleaned rooms," they would say "that I am on the front line of infection control and improving patient outcomes." Through their focus on improving the room turnover and cleaning process and adherence to best practices, they would see themselves as literally helping to save lives! In addition to Hoshin planning helping to achieve organizational goals and objectives, it provides significant relevance to the daily tasks that staffs do. Rather than just "doing work," they are contributing to something "greater" and have relevance and significance beyond just the superficial interpretation of their daily work.

To get to this level of significance, relevance and meaning is not easy, but it is well worth the journey. Some of you may be thinking "we already do goal setting and we have this taken care of." To this, I will say that you should take a second look! Most organizations do annual goal setting, but it is essentially done "TO" your employees and organization, with a very top-down "deployment" approach that leaves staff feeling that the goals are just words on a page with little or no meaning. Most of us have personally experienced this, as the authors definitely have. We have sat down with our boss and set goals for ourselves (such as personal development) and had goals handed down to us (to decrease cost, increase sales, etc.) and then went back to our normal jobs for the next year. At our annual review, our boss takes out our goals and neither they nor the employee has looked at them during the intervening year. Your review is basically dependent on whether or not your boss likes you. The goal setting was a fundamentally useless exercise and didn't drive any action, problem solving, or prioritization over the entire year. You just "did your job" and reacted to what happened on a daily basis; it was rather haphazard and primarily focused on reaction and "firefighting." With such a system (or a lack thereof), it is no wonder that many executives scratch their heads and wonder why their organizations aren't progressing toward their goals or achieving what is needed to prosper and grow. With this sort of broken system persisting for many years, eventually the accumulated organizational dysfunction and lack of direction has accumulated in enough waste and inefficiency that cuts are necessary to stay profitable or survive (see Figures 6.1 and 6.2).

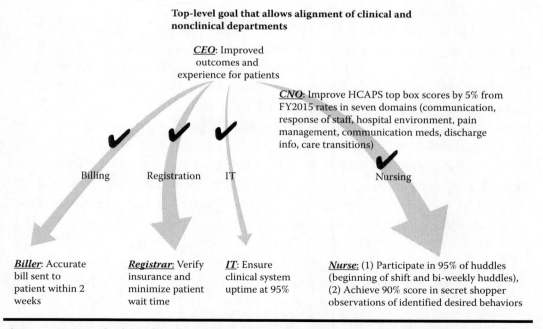

Figure 6.1   Goal of Hoshin: Most areas are able to align and translate meaningful goals at all levels.

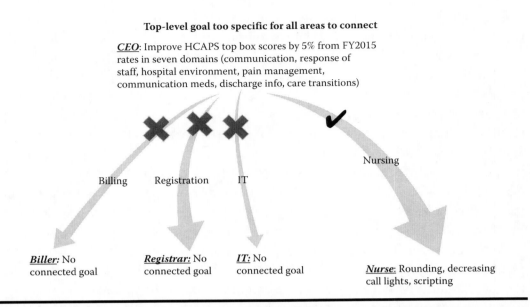

Top-level goal too specific for all areas to connect

CEO: Improve HCAPS top box scores by 5% from FY2015 rates in seven domains (communication, response of staff, hospital environment, pain management, communication meds, discharge info, care transitions)

Billing   Registration   IT

Nursing

Biller: No connected goal

Registrar: No connected goal

IT: No connected goal

Nurse: Rounding, decreasing call lights, scripting

Figure 6.2   Without Hoshin: Goals only allow a single (or small number) of departments to align to an overly specific or targeted top-level goal.

As these cuts take place, morale plummets, our best staff leaves for more promising organizations, and a "death spiral" often persists for years to come, not a desirable path to take!

With Hoshin planning and LDM in place and actively being deployed, your organization goes from passively playing "defense" to playing "offense" and building for the future and having the skills, infrastructure, and culture to get there. Your staff will know the "why" behind the "what," and the leadership rounds and leader daily discipline will add discipline and accountability that keep focus on these critical goals throughout the year. Also, the translation of the Hoshin planning goals to the LDM board will add the "why" behind the "what" to the focus of the LDM boards, what processes and issues are being looked at, the rationale behind the numerical goals, and other factors as well.

To effectively deploy and integrate Hoshin planning into your organization, there are a significant number of detailed aspects that must be put into place for it to be effective, which will be covered in the following sections. Don't be overwhelmed with thinking that all of these need to be put into place right away! As with most aspects of building a holistic Lean system, it requires a long-term perspective, trial and error, refinement of terminology, and integration with technical and social systems. These different aspects require discipline, reinforcement, oversight, and empowering staff, which are often an organizational and cultural challenge that must be overcome over time.

Setting S.M.A.R.T. Goals

The S.M.A.R.T. Goal framework is a very effective framework for helping to educate staff on setting effective and meaningful goals, and avoiding many of the common pitfalls that result in meaningless, unaligned, and ineffective goals. We will go through these one at a time to better understand what they are and why they are important.

- ■ *Specific*: Goals should be clearly written, straightforward, and define what you are going to do. An effective way to evaluate this qualitatively is in how briefly and concisely the goal is written, often a long series of statements and adjectives is a sign that the goal is ambiguous and not well defined, just like with an A3 problem statement, a short, clear, and concise goal statement is a sign that a significant amount of thought and "distillation" has been done to get to the core, specific goal.
- ■ *Measurable*: Goals should have some objective way to evaluate whether the goal has been achieved, or if progress has been made to the goal. This is a challenging aspect of goal setting that often becomes a stumbling block, especially in healthcare. When goals are set that say things like "increase," "decrease," or "improve," if there is not a current baseline measure, then these goal terms are meaningless—how can we improve if we don't know where we are now or how to measure? If we improve the process and can only say "it feels better!" or "we know it is better," these are not strong validations of improvement. Another phrase that reflects this is that "we can't improve what we can't measure!" Improvement is also based on experimentation, and without some form of measurement, then we can't do experiments and evaluate the effectiveness of our countermeasures. At the same time, many processes in healthcare don't have readily available (or meaningful!) data, and this can be a stumbling-block for staff setting goals; they sometimes feel like they need perfect or highly defensible data just like problem solving, often "back-of-the-envelope" data that roughly approximates process performance is sufficient and a huge improvement from where we started!
- ■ *Achievable*: Goals need to "thread a needle" between challenging us to improve, but being achievable, and having the leader and the team believe that they are achievable. If we set an overly aggressive goal, then the team feels oppressed by it and doesn't believe that it can actually be accomplished, and it has the opposite effect of motivation: It leaves the teams de-motivated! If it is too easy to achieve, it is not

driving improvement, and it is an exercise in futility. Therefore, it needs to achieve what Toyota calls a "productive level of stress" enough pressure and focus to improve, but not too much or too little both of which result in little or no improvement. This delicate balance is challenging to achieve and takes practice, homework, and discipline, but it pays off handsomely for the staff and organization as a whole.

■ *Results-focused*: Goals should measure improvement or outcomes, not tasks or activities. It is common to see tasks listed as goals, such as "implement," or "complete," which are often loosely tied to some improvement focus. Unfortunately, this is essentially like skipping "diagnosis" and "symptom" on an LDM board, and jumping straight to "treatment plan." By doing this, we are not setting ourselves up for "experimenting," which is absolutely critical to both goal setting and LDM. Our "treatment plan" is the experiment to improve something. If we are doing an "experiment" without linking it closely to something measurable that we are trying to improve, then there is no feedback loop. We are just "guessing" with tasks that may or may not be improving what we want to improve. We may very well be implementing changes that add cost, complexity, and may not be improving anything, and this would mean that our goals are actually working against the organization, which we absolutely don't want!

■ *Time-bound*: Goals need to be clearly tied to a time line for implementation, incremental goal attainment, and allowing for uncertainty of effectiveness of the tasks or countermeasures identified to achieve the goal. If there is no clear time line tied to the goal, then it is likely to be procrastinated on until close, until the end of specified time-period, with daily operational demands getting in the way. If we spread out the time line over the entire year, we are assuming that everything will go exactly to plan, which rarely occurs in most organizations (or in life!). Therefore, we should set a more aggressive (but achievable) time line to achieve the goal earlier than otherwise necessary, assuming that not everything will go to plan, which will allow us time to do problem solving and identify new or modified countermeasures to try plan–do–study–act (PDSA) to figure out a new path to achieving the goal. Include in this time line regular meetings with your manager/supervisor, as this will help hold yourself (or your direct report) accountable, and results in the normal human behavior of increasing the intensity (and progress) of work toward a goal before a "tollgate" meeting.

Now that we have covered the basic S.M.A.R.T. goal framework, we want to go into more detail on a few related aspects of this to emphasize critical aspects of goal setting and alignment.

Setting Goals to "Strive for," Not Tasks!

Our goals should be something to "strive" for, which means there is uncertainty to how we will achieve it (this is good!). Lexus has arguably the best statement that epitomizes this concept: "The relentless pursuit of perfection." The concept of striving and relentlessly striving toward something is absolutely critical to Hoshin planning and continuous improvement in general. Part of this is the fact that we live in a very dynamic and ever-changing world. Theoretically, if the world was static and didn't change, we could "achieve perfection" with enough time and focus. Fortunately (or unfortunately, depending on how you look at it), the world is ever changing, as is the environment, regulation, competition, market, staff, leadership, and other factors; so continuously improving is essential to even maintain the "status quo." Therefore, setting goals to "strive for" instead of tasks to accomplish aligns very closely with continuous improvement, problem solving, and LDM.

Therefore, if we focus on tasks, we may complete all of these, and accomplish nothing! This is just like "jumping to the right-hand side" of an A3! A worst case (and common outcome) is even worse when we invest resources or add process steps or work that doesn't eliminate waste or improve the process, and actually adds steps, expends resources, and/or adds complexity. This means that we would have been better off doing nothing at all than doing what we did—the opposite of Lean/Toyota Production System (TPS) thinking!

If we focus on setting goals to strive for, and identify tasks that we think will help (address the root causes), it is a much more effective way to get better. We focus our efforts on gathering data on identifying the "gap" between where we are and where we want to be, on identifying the root causes, and then sequentially experiment with trying different countermeasures to move closer to this goal, we have set up an environment of A3-thinking and experimentation and iterative PDSA problem solving to move us toward our goal in a purposeful, effective, flexible, and high-impact way, as long as we "trust the process."

Alignment/Translation ("Why" and "What")

At this point, it is critical that we take a step back from the goals that we are working on, and ask a more fundamental question: (1) Are our goals aligned and meaningful in terms of moving the organization toward its overall goals and (2) are these goals further translated to each level of the organization so that they are measurable and meaningful (and S.M.A.R.T.!)? If not, then setting goals that are only S.M.A.R.T. and not aligned or translated will just result in haphazard, disconnected, and often meaningless work that results in little or no organizational progression toward their strategy and goals. Therefore, S.M.A.R.T. goals that aren't aligned and translated are anything but "smart" goals!

Organizations commonly set strategic/long-term goals and vision, but don't translate these in a meaningful way throughout the organization all the way to the front line. If you ask most senior leaders what the organizational strategy is, they can usually tell you many or all of them. If you ask a mid-level manager or director what these are (or ask any detail), your success rate drops dramatically, especially if you ask them how they can personally impact these on a daily basis! If you continue farther down through the organization and eventually get to front-line supervisors and front-line staff, they are very unlikely to know what these strategies and long-term goals are, and even less likely to know how they can impact these on a daily basis. You usually get a "deer in the headlights" look from these staff, which is the most powerful argument for the critical need for Hoshin planning in an organization! If an organization sets lofty goals and an aggressive strategy to realize these goals, but doesn't do the translation or have staff set S.M.A.R.T. goals, then it is essentially setting itself up for failure! Another way to describe this is the phrase "hope is not a plan!" Without investing the time or effort to align and translate these goals, they are "hoping" that they manifest themselves in actionable behavior throughout the year, which is a recipe for failure! One of the fundamental Lean wastes is not utilizing the creativity and problem solving of our staff, and if we (through inaction) don't utilize the creativity and problem solving of our staff throughout our organization to move toward achieving our strategy, goals, and long-term plan, then this is a systemic and chronic manifestation of this fundamental waste! Given that healthcare is even more biased toward staff (as opposed to equipment and other forms of cost/capital) with staffing cost representing that vast majority of expenses on an ongoing basis, the magnitude of this waste is even more severe than in some other industries.

Every person in the organization needs to have goals translated in a meaningful way so that they know how their work and daily activities help support organizational goals. Without this translation to meaningful, S.M.A.R.T., countable goals, they serve almost no purpose and can even be counter-productive in many respects. When goals are effectively translated throughout an organization, and linked to LDM, then the impact can be profound and powerful! Leaders can walk through an organization, from the top board to the front-line boards (and every level in-between) and see how the strategic goals of the organization have been effectively translated and are being actively implemented (active problem solving and experimentation!) Also, leaders can round and assess the health of their strategy deployment: where are goals actively progressing and being worked on and where are they not? This provides a highly effective "early warning system" for leaders that are actively engaged in this way rather than waiting until the end of the year when it usually becomes evident that goals or strategy are not proving effective or impacting the organization in the intended way when it is too late to do anything about it! When leaders regularly do this, they are able to do "course corrections" midyear and actually have a meaningful impact on goal attainment throughout the year.

This "early warning system" is also highly effective at helping to compensate for a shift that has been happening in healthcare for several decades: the "flattening" of the organizational structure, and the accompanying reduction in management "bandwidth." Span of control and having some extra capacity for leadership engagement, problem solving, support, and staff development are critical aspects of Toyota's organizational structure, and aspects of this have been "withering" in healthcare for decades. To control cost, front-line supervisors, leads, and other levels of midlevel management have been disappearing, sometimes resulting in a supervisor or director having up to (literally) 150 direct reports! With this dilution of management, and the accompanying number of "fires to fight," the pressures on midlevel and senior managers have increased significantly, so it is even more critical for them to be able to make effective use of their time in a way that is meaningful and impactful to the organization (rather than just monitoring budgets, dealing with human resource [HR] issues, and "fighting fires"). By having the managers round on these boards, they can "zero in" on the major gaps and where they can have the biggest impact as managers to help encourage, support, and break down barriers for their teams, and not expend energy trying to help teams that are already making great progress. This system allows our leaders to really make the best use of their time and focus their energies, which is absolutely critical in the modern healthcare environment/hospital!

To illustrate what a "Hoshin-like" translation of goals would look like (in terms of a personal front-line staff connection of a high-level goal to their daily tasks); we will look at one of the most audacious goals that has ever been set:

> *I believe that this nation should commit itself to achieving the goal, before this decade is out, of landing a man on the moon and return-ing him safely to the earth. No single space project in this period will be more impressive to mankind, or more important for the long-range exploration of space.*

> **—President John F. Kennedy, Address to Congress on Urgent National Needs, May 25, 1961**

This was one of the most ambitious goals that has ever been articulated, and set in motion a tremendous investment in research, time, energy, resources, and national pride. Beyond the obvious technical and other aspects of this, one would wonder what a front-line staff member not focused on the core technical work would see as their role.

As previously mentioned, when President Kennedy visited the space center in Cape Canaveral, Florida, he asked a janitorial staff member what his job was expecting a very normal response such as "I clean the floors or I take out the garbage." The janitor responded with "I am helping to put a man on the Moon!" This is a historical example of a high-level strategic or long-term goal being translated (culturally) to a front-line staff member, who helped elevate the staff member's thinking beyond just viewing their seemingly mundane tasks and instead linking them to the high-level goal putting a "man on the Moon!" A fundamental tenet of the Toyota production system is "respect for people," and appreciating the significance and contribution of the seemingly mundane tasks and activities of staff into a greater context is a great example of the potential power of translation and alignment of goals. With each staff member seeing the greater significance of their daily tasks, as well the significance of the potential impact of improving the effectiveness of their daily tasks, the organizational results that could be achieved over time are undeniable!

> *A general is just as good or just as bad as the troops under his command make him.*

> **—Douglas MacArthur**

To make this more applicable to healthcare, let us explore what this sort of translation would look like in healthcare. Most hospitals have a goal for minimizing harm, including decreasing their surgical site infection (SSI) rates in the OR. Many ORs leave the translation at something like all staffs in the OR have their personal goals to decrease SSIs. If they meet the goal, they don't have any real ownership in this win other than any financial bonus. If they don't meet this goal, they feel like they are being punished because they don't know what they did or didn't do to cause them to miss this goal. Either way, it is a meaningless goal that is actually counterproductive to the organization's culture and to staff engagement (see Figure 6.3).

Let's now take a look at a hypothetical organization that is the equivalent to the example from Cape Canaveral and President Kennedy's visit. A hospital chief executive officer (CEO) goes into the OR and asks a housekeeper what his job is, and he responds in the following way: "My job is to minimize SSIs, and I am on the front line of protecting patients and ensuring that they don't get infections!" Upon asking more questions, the CEO asks questions about how they minimize SSIs, and finds out that their manager collaborated with

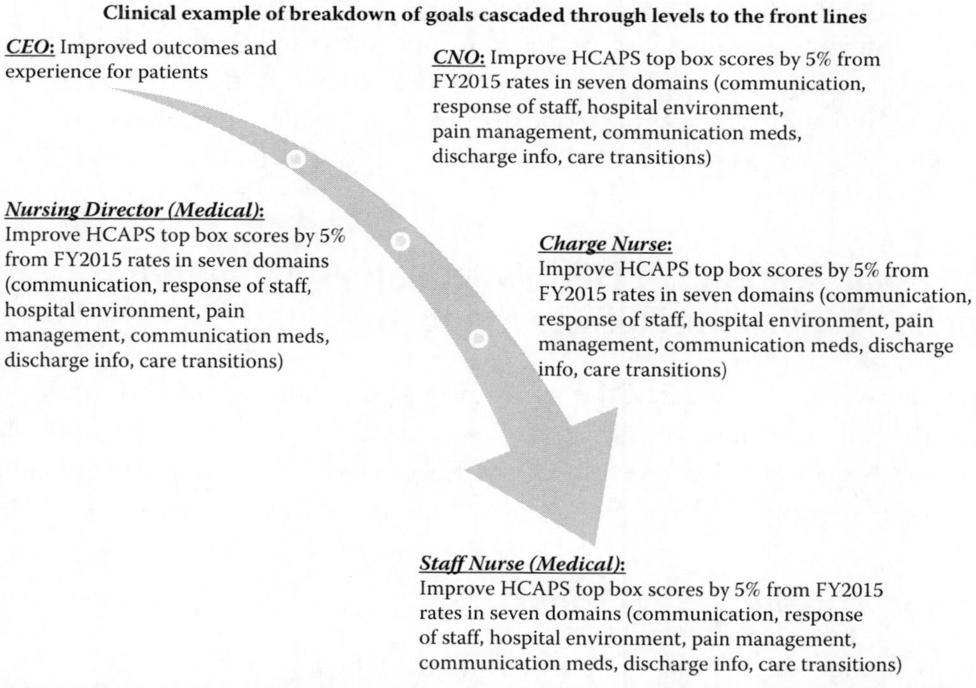

Clinical example of breakdown of goals cascaded through levels to the front lines

CEO: Improved outcomes and experience for patients

CNO: Improve HCAPS top box scores by 5% from FY2015 rates in seven domains (communication, response of staff, hospital environment, pain management, communication meds, discharge info, care transitions)

Nursing Director (Medical): Improve HCAPS top box scores by 5% from FY2015 rates in seven domains (communication, response of staff, hospital environment, pain management, communication meds, discharge info, care transitions)

Charge Nurse: Improve HCAPS top box scores by 5% from FY2015 rates in seven domains (communication, response of staff, hospital environment, pain management, communication meds, discharge info, care transitions)

Staff Nurse (Medical): Improve HCAPS top box scores by 5% from FY2015 rates in seven domains (communication, response of staff, hospital environment, pain management, communication meds, discharge info, care transitions)

Figure 6.3   Hoshin/catchball failure. Lack of translation to the front lines (high-level goal "copied" through multiple levels to the front lines).

the quality and infection control departments to establish standard work and best practices for the housekeeping staff to use, which were integrated onto their LDM boards. Also, their personal goals included metrics on adherence to their standard work and periodic surveillance and validation of their work, including aspects such as adherence to the product-specified dwell time of their antimicrobial solution, cleaning sequence, terminal clean process adherence, and other related (and countable!) aspects of the process. Infection control had helped communicate the evidence-based best practices, which conveyed the "why" behind the "what" to the housekeeping staff. Periodic meetings of small teams of housekeeping managers and front-line staff and infection control helped to continuously improve the process and reinforce the significance of their work (the Hawthorne effect!), as well as senior leader rounding and engagement in the process. Without this sort of support system and alignment, the SSI and overall Harm goal would have been essentially meaningless goals that didn't impact any substantial attainment of the strategy or goal, but instead they were manifested in a living, breathing, and active system that was taking very defensible and real steps toward improving patient care and outcomes and achieving the strategic goals of the organization! Even more importantly, this system helped empower the front-line staff who had never been engaged in this way, and provided them with context, meaning, and significance to their work, which they had never experienced before they truly felt that their work mattered, as well as their ideas and thoughts. It is "respect for people" in action! It is at the heart of the TPS!

Catchball Sessions to Help Negotiate Meaningful Goals: "Where the Rubber Meets the Road!"

Now that we have discussed the mechanics of goal alignment and aspects of goals that are critical (S.M.A.R.T. goals), it is critical to discuss when and where these goals are actually determined and negotiated. These sessions are called "catchball" sessions and will be described in the following sections.

What Is a "Catchball" Session?

Catchball might sound like a game, but it's actually a very simple (but critical) approach to addressing a common and very damaging dysfunction that occurs in almost all organizations when it comes to goal setting and evaluation. When goal setting is done in most organizations between a manager and direct reports, it is not a two-way discussion, it is often goal setting being done "to" the direct report, not a meaningful two-way discussion resulting in the meaningful, translated, and aligned goals that Hoshin planning is seeking to get. This disconnect could prevent the ultimate goal of Hoshin planning from occurring before it even starts so there must be a better way (see Figure 6.4)!

What Takes Place before a Catchball Session?

Before a catchball session takes place, it is important that both the direct report and the manager/supervisor do some preparation beforehand to make the most of their time. If this isn't done, it is possible that much of the first catchball session will be wasted with discussions that could have been addressed prior to the session. If this preparation work wasn't done, then it is still a useful discussion and time to complete this preliminary work during the Hoshin session, but it is highly unlikely that the catchball session will result in finalized goals or meaningful agreement on a plan (due to the lack of preparation beforehand). By doing the prework beforehand, each of the two people at the catchball session have sat down and given some meaningful thought to the goal setting, their questions and concerns about the process, and a vision of what they want to accomplish during the next year.

To properly prepare for a catchball session, the following tasks should be completed, and by whom:

Manager/Supervisor:

■ Completed, or substantially completed, catchball session and form with their manager/supervisor: The catchball/Hoshin process is a linear process, where the goals established at a higher level are cascaded down through the organization. The result of the previous session becomes the "seed" of the next session. If it isn't completed, or the goals weren't done correctly, then the "seed" is unlikely to sprout and bear fruit! Sometimes managers/supervisors look at this process as a "check-the-box" activity and don't do it linearly and skip steps, which results in different catchball sessions with Hoshin goals that aren't aligned or linked, which defeats the whole point of Hoshin!
■ Provide the most recent version of the Hoshin form to your direct report, so they have some idea of your goals going into the first session, so that they have some time to prepare and do some preliminary goal alignment. If the manager's/supervisor's goals aren't provided until

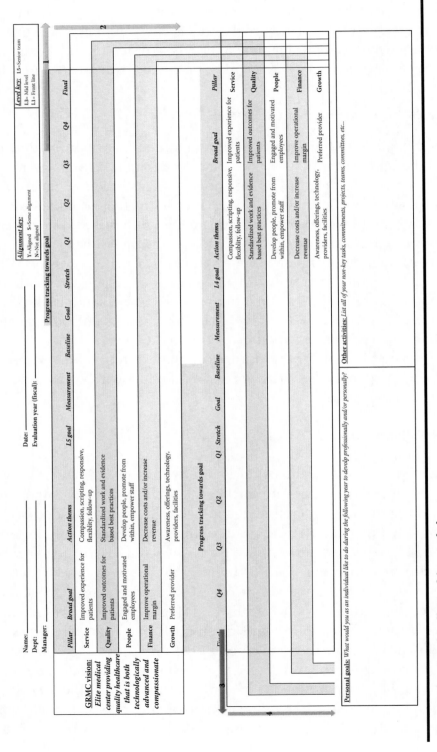

Figure 6.4   Catchball/Hoshin worksheet.

the first session, then much of the session will be wasted with simply reviewing goals that could have been shared beforehand.

■ Prepare a thoughtful explanation of the context and importance of your goals, how they are critical to the organization, and how your direct report is a critical piece of helping you achieve your goals, as well as helping the overall organization to be successful. This succinct, thoughtful, and meaningful narrative is very motivational and an important piece of the Hoshin/catchball process. It helps provide further meaning to the "why" behind the "what" and move farther away from the "check-the-box" mentality that is so rampant in organizations as related to goal setting!

■ Try to anticipate what questions, concerns, pushback, and areas of flexibility you have with your proposed cascading of goals. Some goals are "nonnegotiable" and need to be shared/distributed in a very specific way (such as when an organization is in crisis, or when there is no other way to distribute the responsibility), while other goals are "negotiable." If you go into the session with no flexibility (room for negotiation), then it won't be a catchball session at all and this will defeat the entire point of the Hoshin process! If the staff member feels that this process is being done "to them" rather than in a collaborative way, then the critical buy-in, healthy relationship between a manager and their direct report, and meaningful improvement being driven throughout the year will be lost.

■ Be prepared to explain how the Hoshin/catchball process is different than normal goal setting, why it is important, how the initial catchball sessions will work, how there will be ongoing meetings throughout the year (on a regular basis), and how this will benefit your direct report. Even though there will be organization-wide training and support for Hoshin, there will still be staff that "fall between the cracks" and didn't get the training or education for one reason or another.

Direct Report:

■ Before the catchball session, the direct report should have received their manager's complete (or substantially complete) Hoshin form with the goals of their manager/supervisor drafted. This will give the direct report an opportunity to familiarize themselves with their manager's goals.

- Based on the goals of their manager/supervisor, formulate a preliminary draft of goals that are meaningful to the direct report and align to their manager's/supervisor's goals. These can be very rough, but at least form a foundation for discussion. Along with these goals, they should take notes on their rationale for why these were set the way they were, any questions or concerns they have, and anything else related to this that they would like to discuss during the session.
- A list of "other activities" to discuss with your manager/supervisor to hopefully free up some additional capacity of the direct report away from meaningless, inappropriate, or nonaligned activities. By thinking through this and doing a "brain dump" onto paper beforehand, if there is pushback from the direct report that "there aren't enough hours in the day to do my job AND all of these goals!", that these other activities become a fruitful discussion point on how to come up with a meaningful path forward. These "other activities" will be discussed in more detail in a later section.
- A list of any questions or concerns that the direct report has about the details of the Hoshin/catchball process, the ongoing regular meetings throughout the year to discuss progress toward the goals, and any particular personal or other discussion points.
- Any personal development goals, such as education, cross-training, promotion or leadership opportunities, technical certification, public speaking, or other similar goals. While these sorts of goals are "personal" and do not necessarily align, there may very well be situations where these personal development goals will align with organizational goals or priorities. Also, over time, as your "foundation" of the Toyota house is strengthened, there will be an increasing use of cross-training. As the cross-training is further developed in the organization, it adds a very discrete, tangible, and intuitive personal development goal for employees, as well as naturally integrating with succession planning, which is critical to long-term organizational success.

Now that we have discussed the necessary preparation for a Hoshin/catchball session, we want to discuss in detail what catchball sessions are, how they are different from normal goal-setting discussions, and how to make them successful.

A "catchball" is a physical item (such as a ball or something similar) that is passed between a manager and a direct report as essentially a "talking stick." It is an inanimate object that is used as a coaching tool to help teach a mentor a more productive and positive relationship (specifically during the Hoshin goal setting process). If a manager and a direct report have a healthy, trust-based relationship, then during goal setting and negotiation session, the direct report will feel open to "pushing back" against their boss's goal, and the boss will feel comfortable negotiating and discussing their needs and shared goal that they are asking their direct report to help with. If they don't, it is more of a one-way discussion, with the direct report being "told" what their goals are, and with any pushback being "shot down" by their manager. The direct report is having an internal narrative with their boss that is verbalized, such as "that is completely impossible to achieve with everything else I have going on! It doesn't matter anyways . . . my boss won't ask about these goals until next year and I know that he likes me, . . . so I will get a good evaluation. Also, there are no bonuses anyways, so my evaluation doesn't matter and there is no real promotion opportunity for me, so I really don't care." With one of the core Lean wastes being "not utilizing employee creativity" and the tremendous intelligence, experience, education, and knowledge in a healthcare organization, having our staff being discon-nected from strategy and not believing in or working on their goals through-out the year is a tragic waste. It is no wonder that most organizations are so ineffective at goal attainment and weak at achieving their strategic plan! In this "current state," you could make a strong argument that strategic plan-ning without meaningful translation and deployment (Hoshin planning) is a significant organizational waste!

In a true "catchball" session, the catchball is passed back and forth, and whoever is holding the catchball is the only one allowed to speak, without interruption! It helps to prevent the manager or direct report from interrupt-ing the other in a potentially contentious or emotionally charged negotia-tion/discussion of goal setting. It helps to demonstrate a positive two-way discussion and negotiation rather than a one-way "telling" of goals. If the manager and direct report already have a trust-based relationship and there is true, open, meaningful discussion, then the catchball will just remind or reinforce the discipline of this, and over time it will not be necessary. For the dysfunctional manager/direct report relationship, a catchball will be critical, but not by itself! Just like most "artifacts" such as this, if they are not coached and mentored by a mentor (or "sensei"), they will be just that an inanimate object that is meaningless! With an experienced Hoshin coach/mentor facilitating the discussion, they can see when the proper "back and forth" negotiation is taking place, and the coach will help demonstrate and enforce the discipline of the "catchball." At the beginning of the session, the coach/facilitator will describe the catchball process, the "rules of engagement," the use of the catchball, and the fact that there may have to be more than one catchball session. Also, the facilitator will ask about whether the initial goal setting worksheet and thoughts have been done beforehand. Once this has been reviewed, the session is set to begin!

The manager/leader usually starts and describes the goals that they have negotiated with their manager/boss, the context of the organization, and the importance of their goals to the organization's viability, strategy, and future. Also, they will describe how these goals are shared among multiple direct reports, and that there is a "divide and conquer" approach which is critical to goal achievement.

With that completed, the catchball session is set to begin! After the manager/supervisor has conveyed the goals they have and their thoughts on the goals for their report, as well as conveying the contextual information, the "catchball" (a ball, or anything that is meaningful or helps to serve this simple purpose) passes to the direct report, and they now have an opportunity to provide their thoughts, goals, concerns, ideas, and other relevant aspects of the discussion. In a properly prepared-for and executed session, both the manager and the direct report have done their homework (filling out the Hoshin/catchball form). Also, enough information has been shared with the direct report (including the goals of the manager/supervisor that resulted from their catchball session with their manager) to allow them to go into the meeting ready to "push back," modify, challenge, or provide alternatives.

Once they have had an opportunity to fully voice their thoughts and feedback, the "catchball" goes back to the manager/supervisor, who should now have a better understanding of the level of buy-in and engagement of their staff in helping them achieve their goals. If it is a thoughtful and engaged leader, they will next work to help find "middle ground" to get closer to achieving true buy-in, engagement, and ownership of the goals with their direct report, while still working to make sure they are being challenged enough to help move the organization forward toward their strategic goals, as well as develop their direct report (see Figure 6.5 for cascading of Hoshin goals). This development is a critical aspect of a Lean system, as "respect for people" and developing leaders and staff in the organization is arguably at the very heart of Lean/TPS (see Figures 1.1 and 1.2).

With this "people development" aspect in mind, building a Lean system should over time become an increasingly integrated, holistic, and intertwined system. For example, one of the strategic goals of the organization may (and should) be to develop more and more internal process

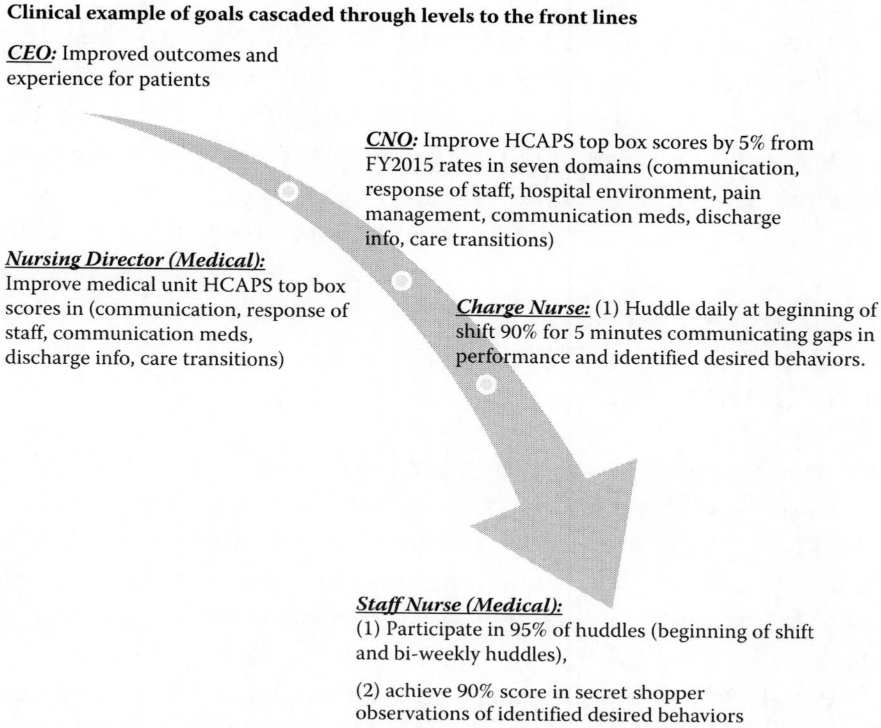

Clinical example of goals cascaded through levels to the front lines

<u>*CEO:*</u> Improved outcomes and experience for patients

<u>*CNO:*</u> Improve HCAPS top box scores by 5% from FY2015 rates in seven domains (communication, response of staff, hospital environment, pain management, communication meds, discharge info, care transitions)

<u>*Nursing Director (Medical):*</u>
Improve medical unit HCAPS top box scores in (communication, response of staff, communication meds, discharge info, care transitions)

<u>*Charge Nurse:*</u> (1) Huddle daily at beginning of shift 90% for 5 minutes communicating gaps in performance and identified desired behaviors.

<u>*Staff Nurse (Medical):*</u>
(1) Participate in 95% of huddles (beginning of shift and bi-weekly huddles),

(2) achieve 90% score in secret shopper observations of identified desired behaviors

Figure 6.5 Detailed example of multilevel cascading of goals from the top of the organization all the way to the front lines.

improvement bandwidth and expertise, as well as developing and hardwiring the LDM system organizational, individual goals with process improvement, waste elimination, and other aspects of a holistic Lean/TPS system. If there was a goal of having a certain "penetration" of LDM boards, or developing a certain level of internal PI/Lean bandwidth and expertise in the organization, then this could be very readily translated through the Hoshin planning process and deployed within an organization. If a manager had 10 different direct reports, he or she might have negotiated a goal with his or her manager to have LDM boards in 6 of the 10 departments by the end of the year, and have these teams huddling a minimum of three times a week. He or she could then pace this out through the year and have a goal to "stand up" an LDM board in his department every two months through the year, resulting in six boards being "up and running" by the end of the year. This would be a S.M.A.R.T. goal that would develop his or her staff and teams, reap organizational and improvement benefits for years to come, and develop the manager by challenging them to get these LDM boards "stood up." It would also integrate closely with the higher level goals and with the manager's senior-level manager having a goal to round with a certain frequency and stay engaged with all of these boards. The manager could also set a goal for LDM leader rounding, development of leader daily discipline documentation/ standard work, doing A3s, 5S projects, and other improvement work. This would be yet another aspect of aligning and supporting a holistic Lean/TPS system!

Other Activities

A "bottleneck" that can occur during the Hoshin process is that very meaningful goals are identified and negotiated between a manager and their direct report, but there are just not enough hours in the day or days in the week to get them done! While the core work they do may be causing this, often there is a much more actionable issue at play that can be brought to the surface and addressed through the Hoshin process!

In almost all organizations, there is an accumulation of random activities, committees, reports, commitments, projects, and other potentially "noncore" work that is often essentially "legacy activities" that have accumulated over the years and never went away. For example, if there was an initiative five years ago that resulted in a report requirement for your direct report, then the periodic generation of this report continued on indefinitely even though the project ended! Or you changed jobs four or five times within the same organization and a small number of random tasks or commitments have followed you from your old role to your new role. Over time, these accumulate to a potentially crippling (but not immediately obvious) level, because your core work may take up 80% of your time, and these random tasks take up the remaining 20%. This remaining 20% of your time is what is absolutely critical for being able to focus on improvement work (such as working toward the organization's strategic goals). Therefore, this random noncritical/ noncore work is getting in the way of allowing you and your direct reports from working on their goal attainment and Hoshin goals or LDM boards or leader rounding, so the unintended cost of these is huge!

To help address this, it is critical for your direct reports (and for you!) to document and review these "other activities," basically brainstorming all of the non-core "things" that you and your direct reports are doing. Then, when you are having the Hoshin session with your direct report, and there is some pushback along the lines of "that is a great goal and I would love to work on it . . . but there are not enough hours in the day!" You can review this list with them, and there will surely be a number of items you can help your direct report stop doing or shift to a more appropriate person (carefully and tactfully) so that they are now able to have the bandwidth to work on their Hoshin goals. Thinking about this in another way, this is also a great way to get buy-in to the Hoshin process, the staff no longer sees this as being a process that adds work through assignment of new or challenging goals, but actually frees up their time and takes some things "off their plate"! Now that is a powerful tool for alignment and cultural transformation!

But How Do We Accomplish These Goals?

Now that we have established and translated meaningful goals and worked to achieve buy-in, the big question is "how do we achieve these goals?" The best, most meaningful and translated goals are just "words on paper" or in a computer and meaningless unless there is motivation, oversight, account-ability, transparency, and meaningful ways to support progress and problem solving toward these goals! This is where the other aspects of LDM, leader rounding, visual management, and the boards come in to play; they are a highly effective and flexible system for supporting, encouraging, and for leaders to stay involved and aware of their team and team members' goal progress and efforts.

There are numerous aspects of Lean and LDM that are highly effective at supporting the aligned and meaningful goals that were created through the Hoshin planning process, and will be explored in the following section:

■ *Monthly meetings with your manager/supervisor to re-assess progress toward goals, identify barriers and next steps, and stay focused on improvement:* All of us (including myself) sometimes fall into a bad habit of procrastination, and only working on "what is in front of us" at the moment. With something like annual goals, it is easy to forget about, or deprioritize these until we are "under the gun" after almost all of the year has gone by and our next review is upon us! At this point, it is really too late, as well set S.M.A.R.T. goals can't be accomplished overnight and require a lot of experimentation, hard work, and problem solving. By doing something as simple as setting up regular monthly meetings with your manager/supervisor, it keeps it "on our radar" and helps maintain a "productive level of stress" to keep moving forward on the goals. At these regular meetings, barriers, progress (or lack thereof), changes in personal, organizational, or other priorities, and other relevant topics are discussed. It helps maintain a more regular focus on the goals, minimizes the amount of time between discussions, maintains a more healthy ongoing relationship between a staff member and their manager, and moves away from the "gotcha" cycle of not looking at goals more than once per year and then having very difficult and awkward discussions at the end of the year (where the manager may be in trouble for not achieving their goals, and then the direct report is under attack from the manager, who sent a strong signal to their direct report that this wasn't a priority because it hasn't been asked about since the last meeting).

If you are a manager/supervisor, you are probably thinking at this point "sure, that sounds great, but who has time to meet with each of their direct reports every month to go over goals? I have so much going on and so many crises, that I can barely get through the day!" You are exactly right! Right now you can't, because problems are rising to their highest level (you!) to be solved rather than being solved at the lowest level possible, with only select problems rising to your level to be solved. This is because you don't have an LDM system in place! LDM is highly effective at facilitating problems to be solved at their lowest level possible, thus freeing up managers and supervisors to focus their efforts on developing and supporting their staff, working on strategic and innovative initiatives, growing the business, and improving processes. This is what managers and supervisors (leaders) should be focusing on, rather than the "firefighting" that is currently getting in the way of doing these critical activities! One of the fundamental Lean wastes is not utilizing the creativity and experience of our staff (people) and developing an LDM system helps target this waste, but it also frees up our managers/supervisors to be true leaders rather than firefighters! Surprisingly, eliminating the waste of not utilizing our employees creativity also results in eliminating much of the waste of not utilizing our leader's creativity and problem-solving ability and talents, which they likely have, and was one of the reasons that they were promoted and selected to be a leader in your organization!

With problems being solved at lower levels, having an escalation system in place from the LDM boards, and staff working on their goals throughout the year, all of a sudden our managers and leaders will have much of their time freed up and they will have time to meet with their staff on a monthly basis to review goals, round on LDM boards,

develop their best staff as their "lieutenants"/successors, and growing/
developing the business. Remember, at its core it is a fundamental shift
from playing "defense" to "offense" through (1) problem solving rather
than firefighting, (2) moving problem solving to its lowest level, (3) freeing up our supervisors/managers to be true leaders, and (4) focusing on
improving and growing the business rather than just treading water!

■ *Integrate improvement efforts with LDM boards, 90-day action plans,
and work on achieving goals as a group/team continuously over the
entire year:* In addition to the monthly meetings we just discussed, we
want to focus as much of the problem solving as possible into small
groups and problem-solving teams. There is rarely a problem that a single person can identify, problem solve, and fix on his or her own. Also,
during the Hoshin goal-setting process, many of the goals are shared
between multiple staff (not unique to each staff member), so these are
a natural fit as an improvement topic for their LDM board, so that all of
the members of a team that share a similar (or dependent) job continuously meet as a team and meet with their supervisor/manager throughout the year to work toward achieving their goals. Sounds great, doesn't
it? Rather than a year of just "doing the work" and "fighting fires," the
year is spent working together collaboratively as teams and with managers, and being on the "offense" improving and growing the business!

Also, the monthly Hoshin meetings between managers and staff
don't have to be all one-on-one meetings. If staff that report up to a
manager all share a lot in terms of annual goals, the regular meetings
with the staff on their Hoshin goal progress could (and should) over
time be closely aligned to their LDM board, so hardwiring the LDM
leader rounding to regularly attend their staff's LDM problem-solving
sessions would serve the same purpose as this, updates, feedback,
escalation items (help), adjustment of goals, and the leader's attendance showing the staff that this is critically important to the manager/
supervisor (because they are there and asking!). The one-on-one
meetings with staff could be more focused on individual goals (such as
personal development, education, cross-training, etc....) and occur less
frequently (such as quarterly instead of monthly). This would reinforce
the concepts of integration and how critical LDM leadership rounding is
to the development of a LDM system!

While most of this discussion has been on the problem-solving focus
of LDM and Hoshin, there is often an equally important and challenging aspect of work (and goal achievement) that is often a significant

gap in organizations that don't deal with problem solving directly, but can relate to annual goals and Hoshin. There is often a significant amount of discrete task-work for new projects and initiatives that must be completed in a specific sequence or by a certain date to prepare for an inspection, certification, to establish a new line of business, or another related activity. Many (or most) of these tasks don't require problem solving per se, but they do require ongoing focus and attention to help fight the procrastination tendency that basically all individuals and organizations suffer from to some extent. Remember the prioritization board that we discussed earlier (Figure 3.10)? This prioritization board is a great mechanism for helping to keep teams focused on these tasks throughout the year to help them achieve their Hoshin goals and improve their organization through completion of these tasks that have been identified as being important to the organization's goals and objectives. If a department is having daily LDM problem-solving sessions, perhaps one of these LDM problem-solving sessions could be focused on these tasks and the prioritization board. In these prioritization LDM sessions, the primary problem solving would be on the sequencing, timing, and relative prioritization of these tasks, as well as team assignments, deadlines, and escalating items up the chain of command for help where it is needed. The continued focus and regular discipline of focusing on these tasks will be a tremendous help and facilitator to ensure continued progress and completion of these tasks. Also, the LDM leader rounds will reinforce the importance of these tasks to the organization and act as a further motivator, as well as being a regular and natural opportunity for escalation items to be presented and discussed with their leader!

■ *Focus on "back-of-the-envelope" measurements that are not time consuming but allow you to understand the effectiveness of changes*: In order to achieve the Hoshin goals, it is critical (except with the project management/tasks previously discussed) to stay away from just guessing and making changes that may or may not be effective. We want to focus on the fundamental PDSA cycle, which is at its core a form of scientific method. Without data or a feedback mechanism to test the effectiveness of our countermeasures (i.e., changes we are trying out), then we are just guessing and there is a fundamental breakdown of our LDM system! We need to keep refocusing our teams on "back-of-the-envelope," or counting/frequency data that isn't perfect but allow us to gain enough insight or understanding of a process or issue that either requires extremely time-intensive data gathering to get perfect data, or where there is no data available. Teams often default to thinking that we need perfect data (or large-sample-size data), which is probably driven by previous managers who challenged or questioned the validity of less than perfect data they saw. This then drives our teams to skipping data gathering all together and just "acting" without validating. To avoid this trap, we as leaders need to encourage our teams to gather this back-of-the-envelope data as much as possible. During the LDM leader rounding, as well as during the periodic Hoshin meetings, it is critical that we always ask them for some form of at least rudimentary quantification of the effectiveness of what they are doing. If they aren't doing this (either teams or individuals), it is a perfect "early warning system" to identify a breakdown in the health of the LDM system and a great opportunity to step in as a leader and help to reinforce this critical gap in their thinking and problem solving.

Given the criticality of data to problem solving and goal achievement, reinforcing and encouraging teams to become experts at data gathering is critical. Using their creativity and problem solving to develop innovative and novel ways to measure and count problems unlocks many new and exciting opportunities for problem solving.

■ *Form small, multidisciplinary teams to help tackle problems in a collaborative way:* As teams continue to practice their LDM sessions at their boards, a variety of different problems will "bubble to the surface" that can't be addressed "within the four walls of their department." Some of these will be escalation items that need to go to their manager, some will be large, multidisciplinary teams (that need strong leadership and facilitation), while others are small to medium sized problems that require a multidisciplinary approach and involve outside departments. In most healthcare organizations, these small to medium sized problems don't normally result in collaborative team problem solving at best they may result in standing meetings that don't accomplish anything. With the clearly defined Hoshin goals now in place, and teams becoming practiced in team-based A3 problem-solving approaches (using the simplified A3 structure inherent in the LDM board structure), they are set up for success to problem solve in a meaningful way (alignment through Hoshin, and meaningful problem solving through A3 thinking).

Finding the Right Balance and Understanding the "WIIFM" Principle—Using Hoshin and Catchball!

Goal Setting and Catchball: Negotiating Goals for Improvement and Buy-in

Goals should follow the S.M.A.R.T. goal framework (described previously) as closely as possible, and the catchball process strives to strike a balance between inherent biases and tensions that exist between a manager/supervisor and a direct report, which will be discussed in the next section. At the core of this is a significant component of the "what's-in-it-for-me (WIIFM)" principle . . . ?"

Managers naturally want to set aggressive "stretch" goals to drive the greatest improvement, but sometimes these are too aggressive and the team feels that they are unachievable, which is demotivating. The manager/supervisor thinks that by mandating it, it will somehow happen on its own, and doesn't realize that this makes the entire goal-setting process meaningless if the direct report doesn't see it is achievable or meaningful. The WIIFM for the manager is that they want to "achieve" and meet their goals, which will make them look like strong and effective leaders in the organization, and explains why they often set overly aggressive (and likely unachievable) goals for their staff. Therefore, the WIIFM is actually being sabotaged by their overzealousness! If they truly want to "achieve" and look like strong leaders for their organization, they need to learn a new way of leading, goal setting, and management, which is LDM integrated with Hoshin/catchball!

Just like their managers/supervisors, direct reports rely heavily (just like any rational person would) on the WIIFM principle, but from a different perspective. When a manager/supervisor sets an overly aggressive (and likely unachievable) goal that the direct report doesn't believe in, they see this (rightfully so), as setting them up to fail. Therefore, they really have little or no incentive to work hard on achieving this goal. If they put in the extra effort to do this, they will still likely fail. Based on past organizational experience, they probably believe (rightfully so) that the organization and their manager's/supervisor's goals and priorities will shift or they won't think this is a priority much longer. Therefore, it is in the direct report's best interest to basically ignore the goal. This doesn't help the manager/supervisor, or the organization as a whole, so this lack of engagement and buy-in of the direct report short-circuits the whole goal setting process, and ensures that the WIIFMs for the manager/supervisor and the organization are not realized.

Therefore, it is in the best interest of the entire organization to embrace the Hoshin/catchball process, and that there is a lot of "WIIFM" for all involved!

With regards to employee-established goals, which are at the opposite extreme of managers setting unrealistic or unachievable goals, there is another dysfunction that relates to the WIIFM principle. Some managers/ supervisors probably realized a while ago that the goal-setting process is substantially meaningless in their organization, and simply have employees set their own goals, which only get a cursory review from their manager/ supervisor. When this occurs, the WIIFM for the direct report is to "set themselves up for success" in terms of the bureaucracy of their healthcare organization's HR system, but not move the overall organization toward their goals or toward meaningful improvement. That is, they want to set goals that are very achievable, but this sometimes leads to just "tasks" or goals that don't drive improvement. They basically "set the bar" very low and have goals that they know they will achieve (or already achieved); so that at the end of the year they will meet their goals, get their raise, or get a promotion. With the goals being self-set by the direct report, this is very rational for the direct report; honestly, many of us would do the same if we were given the chance, because we all want to succeed and get an "A"!

Finding Middle Ground

Therefore, we can see that neither manager/supervisor/direct report-established goals are going to lead to meaningful alignment, achievement, and improvement; the WIIFM principle for each of these two parties sabotages the process and ensures that nobody wins in the long run.

The Hoshin/catchball process is a highly effective way of finding this middle ground, and over time, all members of the organization start to see more WIIFM in the new process! The "catchball" process is a way for negotiating the critical "middle ground" between staff and leadership for goals that drive improvement, but are achievable and the staff believes in. It is striking that natural balance of "productive stress" that is critical, as too little stress leads to apathy and "going through the motions," while too much stress is crippling. Organizations that commit to learning and implementing this new Hoshin process, integrated with an active LDM system, begin to see that the only way to "achieve" and be on the "offense" as an organization is to utilize the creativity and problem solving of their leaders and staff, establishing and staying focused on long-term goals that don't waver. If the goals aren't set effectively, establishing a productive level of stress for the direct report coupled with buy-in from both parties and ongoing, flexible, and supportive engagement by the manager/supervisor, then it is an exercise in futility.

Another critical note on effective goal setting is that to be successful at this requires investigation, "number crunching," and a meaningful two-way discussion with your manager. Just like with LDM boards, there is often a "vacuum" of meaningful data related to critical organizational problems and improvement opportunities, and this affects goal setting as well. It is critical that we set data-driven goals as much as possible (remember the S.M.A.R.T. criteria we discussed earlier?), and the catchball back and forth with the manager/supervisor and the direct report needs to include discussion of how to effectively (and efficiently) measure the improvement goals we are setting. If we don't focus on this, then we are likely to get to the end of the year and say "the process feels better" but we can't quantify it. This isn't a good way to run a healthcare organization or to develop our people, and it rarely leads to goal achievement. We need to encourage the "back-of-the-envelope" data collection that we discussed earlier, as this will pay off handsomely in terms of effective goal setting and achievement of goals. Also, during the periodic update meetings that we will have throughout the year, we can discuss these metrics when asking the question "how are we doing on goal XX?" It also sets these goals up for being a great fit for the LDM boards, as well as for the scientific method/PDSA-style experimentation that is critical to improve all but the most trivial of process issues.

LDM Tip: Using LDM to support a "productive level of stress:" Stress in one form or another is pervasive in organizations, as we know all too well! Like most things in life, stress is either good or bad, in different situations it can be either (or even both!). For example, no stress at all can lead to almost complete and total apathy, which makes it difficult to be productive or get anything done (think of being on vacation too long, productivity goes down and it is hard to go back to work!). At the opposite extreme is crippling stress, such as an impossible project, an unreasonable boss, or completely conflicting and contradictory goals! In this situation, the stress can be crippling and lead to no positive outcome, burnout, health problems, or a host of other problems. Therefore, we need to find the right balance between "crippling" high stress and "apathy-inducing" lack of appropriate stress—we will call this "productive stress." This is a principle that Toyota uses in their organization to challenge individuals, teams, and the organization as a whole to improve and move forward, without burning out the organization through losing their most important asset due to "crippling" stress (remember, people are Toyota's, and your organization's #1 asset!). When we don't have clearly defined goals or a system for teams to use for problem solving and getting support from their leaders, they are guaranteed to go through long periods of little or no stress (and no improvement!) because there is no pressure or oversight or guidance from their manager (thus resulting in not enough stress). After this period of no stress, the organization is likely to go through a period of crippling stress due to a financial crisis or overly ambitious project, where unachievable goals are set, as well as the individuals and teams being ill equipped to deal with these challenges because of a lack of LDM. Therefore, the organization seesaws between too little and too much stress, which we have all experienced in our organization. LDM provides a steady cadence of problem solving, improvement, leader engagement and support, goal setting and achievement, and alignment. This helps to stabilize the organization through a continual focus on improving processes, eliminating waste, and solving problems, so there is a decreased likelihood of organizational and departmental crises, and when they do occur, they are less severe. When a crisis does occur, you have an active, responsive, and effective LDM system composed of engaged and visible leaders, highly effective and responsive problem-solving teams and individuals, and an overall system that is ready to deal with the challenges that they are faced with! And most importantly, this LDM system maintains the productive level of stress that helps protect our most valuable asset— our people—from layoffs, burnout, and other negative outcomes.

Now, we will discuss a step-by-step approach to deploying Hoshin planning and linking it to your LDM system:

1. Conduct top-level strategic goal setting as early as possible; invest as much time as you can as early as possible and receive as much feedback as you can! Most organizations wait too long to do this, and then take too long, and this doesn't give 95% of the organization enough time to work on their goals. If you don't do a good job at the top, it is "garbage in/garbage out" throughout the organization, as everybody is using these top-level goals in one way or another to translate, link,

and cascade throughout the organization! If you do a great job at the top level and take too long, then most of the catchball sessions will just be "check-the-box" activities and will be largely wasteful for the organization.

2. Develop a disciplined schedule for deploying Hoshin planning throughout your organization, allowing sufficient time for each level to have multiple catchball sessions. Allow some "slack" time at the end just in case the process takes longer than expected, which it likely will early on!

3. Train all leaders and managers in the organization in the Hoshin/catchball process so that they deeply understand the process and how it is different than normal goal setting. Demonstrate (with role playing) good and bad catchball sessions, good and bad examples of filling out the Hoshin alignment form, periodic (quarterly) goal-review sessions, and so on.

4. Work with HR to integrate and streamline the "mechanics" of Hoshin with their existing goal setting/performance evaluation systems (or working to get appropriate software or systems to support Hoshin), and develop training and support resources for deploying in the organization. If there is an electronic annual goal setting and performance management system (which most hospitals above a certain size will have), evaluate its ability to align and translate top-level goals all the way through an organization, update goals and show progress (or lack thereof) during the year, flexibility to adapt to unique departmental goals and challenges, and view progress and effectiveness of Hoshin/catchball sessions as well as goal attainment and regular meetings. If the current system is not supportive of this, don't delay starting the Hoshin process! Develop a manual Hoshin system of paper forms or another similar system to facilitate the process, and then deploy in key areas for the first year or two. As soon as this system gap is identified begin working on identifying a suitable vendor who has a product that will support your Hoshin efforts, and schedule demonstrations and ask them targeted questions related to the Hoshin process you are working to develop. Once you identify a vendor, budget this (it will be more than worth it!), and continue developing your system until the new system is in place to support. If you find that your paper system (the work-around) is effective and drives meaningful goal setting and alignment and doesn't result in too much additional labor and resources, don't feel compelled to get a fancy electronic system! Just use the system that is already working! Toyota always recommends trying the

"simple/little/no cost" solution first and only going to more sophisticated solutions when the simpler solutions have been ruled out. Do the same in this case!

5. In addition to any electronic goal setting programs, it is critical to develop a Hoshin/catchball form (paper and pencil, just like doing an A3!) that fits with your organization's terminology, pillar goals, and other unique characteristics (see Figure 6.4 for an example of a Hoshin/catchball form). These forms are extremely helpful for facilitating and capturing the real-time catchball discussions that take place. Some people may say that this isn't necessary and is a wasteful "extra step" as we already have a computer program to capture these. The reality is that, especially at first, there is as much struggle and difficulty with the goal-setting software as there is with the catchball form. The last thing we want is for the technology to distract and detract from the meaningful catchball discussion, as having the goals and alignment documented on a paper sheet allows for the struggle with making the goal information in the form to be fit and adapted into the software program. Also, it is very rare that any goal-setting program actually fits the outcome of the catchball session perfectly, so keeping the results of the form on record and updating periodically during the quarterly or more frequent update sessions throughout the year is a highly effective way to further facilitate these discussions. Just like most things with Lean/TPS, we want to always use the lowest technology, lowest cost solution first and only use technology when we are required to do so, or when it genuinely solves a problem that couldn't be solved any other way. Hoshin planning and using pencil, eraser, and paper for the catchball sessions is a perfect example of this principle!

6. Develop multiple Hoshin "super users" who have deep knowledge and experience with the Hoshin, goal setting, and catchball process. These "super users" will serve two primary uses:

   a. Facilitate the critical top-level strategic goal setting, as well as the C-suite/senior executive catchball sessions. These activities are few in number and absolutely critical to the success of the overall initiative due to the nature of org charts being so narrow at the top and spreading out so widely at the bottom. As the goals cascade from "few" to "many," errors or poorly composed or defined goals are amplified as they spread during the Hoshin process.

   b. These "super users" would also serve a critical role as internal coaches/mentors/trainers for the embedded Hoshin coaches. Their much greater level of knowledge and experience would be critical for the embedded coaches to "borrow their learning curve," which is a common and critical "theme" of developing a Lean system—mentorship and guidance is critical! In addition to the mechanics of training/coaching/mentoring the embedded coaches, these "super users" would also be benefitting from this second role as well: There is no better way to learn something yourself than to train, develop, and support others! Also, these "super users" went through the top-level goal setting, so they have critical knowledge/awareness of the top-level organizational goals (and associated context, the "why" behind the "what"), which can be conveyed and used to help support the embedded coaches in their work. These staff may very well (and probably will) be some of our Lean-/TPS-embedded coaches who are cross-trained as the Hoshin super users—the overlap in personalities, temperaments, and systems-thinking with good Lean-/TPS-embedded coaches would be significant (and should be). This also helps support the spread and development of LDM boards, given the long-term alignment of LDM boards with Hoshin goals.

7. Identify and train (through shadowing the Hoshin/catchball "super users" and other forms of instruction and guidance) embedded Hoshin "coaches" to attend/facilitate Hoshin sessions, provide feedback on the sessions, develop leaders and staff in becoming better goal setters and goal translators, and to be overall organizational resources to support and integrate Hoshin. Don't underestimate the importance of this! Just like most things, Hoshin takes practice and is a big change for the organization and individuals within the organization. If it is not mentored and coached, it will just be "wallpaper" in that the forms and systems will just be corrupted to match the old way of goal setting, but with more steps and false pretenses (in this case, it would be better to have not done Hoshin than to do it halfheartedly). These embedded coaches would be located in different divisions, groups, departments, or areas, and would need dedicated time to be developed, and during the major "push" of goal setting would need to have their core positions "backfilled" to allow them sufficient time for this critical role. Even though this might temporarily cause a slight decrease in productivity, it will pay off handsomely for the organization that makes this investment! Another way to simplify this process instead of having departments and areas with (what appears to be) decreased productivity due to the dedicated Hoshin staff is to have

a separate department or charge code set up in the payroll system so that the staff can charge their hours to this different charge code (rather than ambiguously falling into decreased global productivity of the department). This has a second benefit as well: it allows for clear financial quantification of the financial investment in the goal-setting process. This is also a very good approach for charging hours of general Lean-/TPS-embedded coaches, where the issues are the same as having partially dedicated Hoshin coaches: the departments that identify to develop these staff and invest their time are "punished" in the accounting system for doing this, and this acts as a strong disincentive to the departments identifying and investing in their staff. When this counterproductive incentive system is fighting our efforts to develop our best people, our staff who are supposedly 25% "dedicated" to Hoshin or continuous improvement are constantly pulled into the day-to-day crisis management of the department and in actuality end up spending probably only 3%, or at most 10%, of their time working on Hoshin or Lean/TPS efforts, which is not sufficient to give them the requisite experience, knowledge, cycles of learning, or enough bandwidth to meaningfully benefit the organization to the extent intended. With a separate charge-code, the amount of their work in these critical dedicated roles is much easier to quantify, they are likely to be more accountable and be able to "push back" against the pull for daily firefighting needs and for holding the staff more accountable for the outputs/results for their dedicated efforts. These embedded coaches will need to help train and facilitate dozens (or hundreds) of these sessions to become true "masters" of the catchball and goal-setting process, but once they are, their value to the organization on an annual and ongoing basis will be tremendous! Don't forget, this isn't just a "once a year" activity . . . there are quarterly (or more often) review sessions that are a "refresher" on their goals, what has changed in the organization, and their progress (or lack thereof) toward these goals. Therefore, goal setting changes from being a "once a year" activity to being a continuous, ongoing effort (just like LDM boards!) to encourage, align, and support progress toward the organization's strategic goals at all levels of the organization—from the C-Suite/Board of Directors all the way down to the front lines.

8. Now that you have facilitated high-quality top-level goals, trained Hoshin/catchball "super users," worked to set up your Hoshin forms and associated goal setting software, done awareness training for your staff and leaders, and established a time line, you are in a great place to start a more broad roll-out of Hoshin! If your organization is of a

size that is appropriate to be supported by the Hoshin "super users," embedded coaches, and other resources identified and developed for rolling out Hoshin, then you can begin cascading your goals (through facilitated catchball session's—remember, if you just assume that the meetings will go well, you are setting your organization up for failure during the upcoming year and helping to establish new bad habits!). If, like most organizations, you don't have enough dedicated resources to roll out Hoshin organization-wide (which is most organizations, because they under-estimate the time that it will take to do these catchball sessions, especially including the fact that these catchball sessions usually require multiple sessions when first starting Hoshin), there is fortunately a great alternative that is recommended for most organizations, and that is in line with the Lean concept of establishing a "model line." Instead of organization-wide roll-out, you pick a few parts of the organization with strong and committed top-level support, and a strong "chain of command" all the way to the front lines. Make sure you DON'T pick your greatest challenge or an area where there are already deep-seated leadership or management issues! This is an EXTREMELY common mistake that organizations make, with Hoshin and process improvement in general. When an organization is just starting their journey (overall, or with a specific approach), you want to "set yourself up for success" to allow for organizational and individual learning through the exercise, and to have a "go and see" area to demonstrate to the rest of the organization that "this works here . . . not just external examples that the consultant had or that I read about in the book." This is a very powerful change tool! You then take all of the Hoshin/catchball resources that you developed for the organization (but weren't sufficient for organization-wide roll-out) and concentrate them in this one area. Now you have enough resources to effectively support this more focused deployment! Remember, it is all about "quality" rather than "quantity"; we want to have successes and learnings coming from these activities, not just "checking the box"! The senior coach (sensei) will watch and help guide the super users and other coaches, and attend many of these sessions to help facilitate the sessions, as well as to continue mentoring and coaching the super users and embedded coaches. Once the sensei is confident (through real-life Hoshin observations) that the super users and embedded coaches are sufficiently trained and experienced "in the field," then they can let them learn and experience on their own, now that they have a foundational knowledge.

9. After completing this pilot phase of Hoshin/catchball through creating a "model line" and completing the goal setting, conduct a post-deployment "Hansei" (reflection) session to reflect on what worked, what didn't work, and how we could do better next year. This sort of reflection is absolutely CRITICAL! It allows us to continuously improve and adapt, which is critical to any organizational deployment or improvement effort. This would allow us to identify changes to forms, changes to our HR goal-setting system, potentially change to a different software product, identify bandwidth issues with how many coaches we have, establish better time lines for deployment, as well as a litany of other improvements and insights that we can use before we do hospital (or system-wide) deployment. During the next year, these same coaches and support resources will need to be closely monitored and supported to ensure that they continue to have the periodic sessions to review progress, identify successes, as well as identify barriers. As often as possible, you want these sessions to be facilitated by the same coaches who did the initial catchball discussions, because they possess the original context and knowledge of the goals. At the end of the year, doing Hansei (reflection) sessions with staff involved in Hoshin at all levels within this model line will provide an opportunity to help communicate the power and effectiveness of this approach to others in the organization. "Verbatims" or testimonials help communicate (in a peer-to-peer fashion) what the experience was like, that it wasn't something to fear, that it led to increased job satisfaction and organizational "context" and meaning throughout the year, and resulted in "kudos," successes, and positive accolades for the department that "stepped up to the plate" to be open to change, try a different approach, and take a risk. This approach of positive reinforcement is critical! Early adopters "step up to the plate" despite the uncertainty, and there are always departments and leaders who are more "wait and see" and skeptical based on personality, temperament, or negative previous experiences. When they hear that this approach is leading to positive outcomes, accolades to the leaders and staff, and that the organization's leadership is staying committed to this (and it's not just "a flavor of the month"), they are much more likely to be willing to accept and try it.

10. Now that we have had a successful "pilot" of the Hoshin process, we take what we have learned in terms of mechanics/logistics, timing, coaching/support bandwidth, change-management, accountability and ongoing sessions throughout the year, we wrap this all together into a

plan to deploy Hoshin more thoroughly throughout the organization. With enough commitment and resources, you could deploy hospital (or system wide), but you will likely see during the "model line" pilot that it is more resource-intensive at first than originally thought. For example, each of the Hoshin/catchball sessions take several sessions to do correctly and certain areas will be much more difficult to do than others (due to the nature of the work, availability of metrics, difficulties with multiple shifts, or with highly resistant leaders or staff). Setting the top-level goals correctly is often started too late and compresses the time for a huge number of staff to complete their sessions. If this is the case (as it is with most organizations, whether they believe it or not), continue to incrementally roll out the Hoshin to more and more parts of the organization, continuously refining the process, developing your bandwidth to support these efforts, and having a greater and more diverse set of internal examples and "wins" to help build a case for change for others in the organization (who are inherently more resistant than the "early adopters"). By taking this incremental approach, you are getting more wins earlier than you would have with an "all-in" approach, refining your process and bandwidth to properly support the efforts, and constantly reflecting to do better with each successive "wave" of Hoshin/catchball. This is also a highly effective approach given the natural bell curve of people and departments. The early adopters are open to change and embrace the new process. The "middle of the curve" are more neutral and take a wait-and-see attitude, which is supported by the success of the model/pilot line. By the time you get to the "other end of the curve" opposite the early adopters, you have greatly matured the process, support, mechanics, and case studies to make it much more difficult for these staff (who are almost pathologically resistant to change) to not at least try it, especially given that the organization and leadership are now fully engaged and supportive of this approach and it is clear that to not embrace it at this point would reflect very badly on their department and annual performance.

11. Throughout this process of experimenting with Hoshin, deploying it in a pilot/model line, and then broad deployment, you want to be continuously integrating with competing initiatives, LDM boards, leader rounding, quality, and other process improvement initiatives. As with any initiative, they are unlikely to survive alone "in a desert" and be seen as "just one more thing." If they are integrated with other initiatives and seen as being integral to an organization's strategy, survival,

and health, then it is much easier to get appropriate levels of buy-in, support, and engagement. Over time, the content on the LDM boards will align more closely with the Hoshin goals, which are tied to the performance/merit/incentive system, so there is a strong reason for the teams to be doing LDM. For the same reason, there will be strong incentives for leaders to round on the LDM boards and conduct their own LDM sessions, as rounding on these boards will be indiscernible from "going to the Hoshin Gemba" and they will literally be able to walk through their chain of command at any time throughout the year and determine where there is strengths, weaknesses, successes, failures, and opportunities for them (as leaders) to support and engage with their teams. Integrating Hoshin-aligned Lean projects with the LDM boards, is a further three-way alignment that is extremely powerful (LDM board focusing on small/medium problems, Lean projects focusing on large or multidisciplinary issues, and leader rounding, which all reinforce each other). This "weaving" is all part of developing "your organization's way" and not having different initiatives as separate/stand-alone pieces—it is over time integrating all of them into a meaningful whole! (see Figure 6.6).

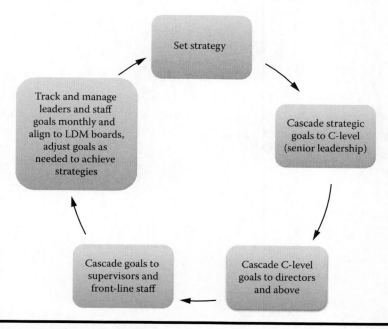

Figure 6.6   Annual Hoshin planning.

LDM Tip: Use LDM to avoid "organizational attention deficit hyperactivity disorder (ADHD):" This may seem like a strange term, but every time we mention the term "organizational ADHD," everybody from senior leaders to front-line staff know EXACTLY what we are talking about! Just like a patient struggling with ADHD, organizations struggle with constantly changing priorities, directions, metrics, leadership styles, and just about everything else! Most organizations are constantly "playing defense" and reacting to what is around them, which results in very short-term thinking and is the opposite of what Lean and Toyota teach us! When we are constantly reacting, there is no consistency of focus, follow-through, or a stable environment to teach and develop our people. Through Hoshin planning, LDM, and fundamental Lean process improvement, long-term thinking, proactive problem solving, aligned goals, leader rounding, Lean project management, and other aspects of the holistic system-building approach that we have described, we are able to get out of this "trap" of short-term thinking that leads to organizational ADHD! Our organization is shifting from being "on defense" to being "on offense," and has sufficient focus, consistence, support, leadership, and stability to cure our organization's chronic ADHD!

Journal

This is your opportunity to process and creatively express your ideas. You can write *questions* you still have, *responses* that were significant to you, or simply *summarize* your thoughts.

   Be creative!

Chapter 7

Lean Projects

Lean projects have traditionally been the starting point for Lean implementations in the hope of quickly proving the value of Lean tools and methods with staff and leadership. As mentioned in the beginning of this book, we believe establishing Lean daily management (LDM) (leader daily disciplines, leadership rounds, and LDM boards) across the organization is the first key step. Establishing LDM first allows leaders and staff to align and engage in their key goals and begin to problem solve around them daily. LDM creates a continuous improvement cadence/rhythm/discipline and practice across the organization. As staff and leaders learn to track, problem solve, and experiment with ideas to attain their LDM board's goals, they will inevitably be pulled to Lean tools.

So if LDM is the first step, do we simply ignore Lean projects? The answer to this question depends on how much commitment you have from senior leadership to implement LDM first. In most organizations, there will be some leaders that prefer to lead with projects and may not see the value of the LDM boards early on. LDM and this book are not meant to be a static model for implementing LDM. The Lean coach and senior leadership team need to assess how to best implement LDM within their organization. This will often result in a "hybrid" LDM implementation with Lean projects (Kaizens in the OR or emergency department) deploying alongside LDM boards, leadership rounds, and leader daily disciplines.

As you launch Lean Kaizen events, value stream mapping (VSM) teams, 5S efforts, and so on try to ensure that each of these project teams use LDM boards, leader daily discipline, and leadership rounds to sustain their Lean project implementations.

At the beginning of the Lean project (chartering phase), build in development of the LDM board, leader rounds, and leader daily disciplines for the key process or departments that will be affected. Build "rounding" into the Lean project schedule from time to time instead of just a traditional sit down project report out/update. Get project teams to get used to reporting results for their projects at their LDM boards. Incorporate project analysis and action items into the LDM board where it makes sense.

Lean A3 Projects and LDM

As your LDM implementation matures, there will be a demand/pull for A3 project support because A3s tend to be the tool of choice for the front lines (focused problem-solving tool). The Lean coach/Lean office will quickly want to train and develop key managers on A3 problem solving so they can support their staff with A3s that start to escalate up to their level and higher. Developing an A3 workshop for key managers to start with some practical coaching as well is a good start. A3 Lean projects (driven from LDM problem solving) will become the way staff and leaders start to prioritize resources.

Many healthcare organizations are already using Lean A3 problem-solving projects in close coordination with their LDM system to prioritize resources and manage the continuous improvement efforts across the organization.

Ideas that staff can implement right away to improve their LDM board goals will always take priority, however, leaders will quickly want to develop the capability of their staff to use the A3 problem-solving process (Figure 7.1).

"VSM" (large-scale change) projects can be used when there is a need for big change. Value streams were typically the starting point for traditional Lean implementations because it forced leaders and staff to align themselves to key processes or service lines and the patient/customer first and foremost. VSM teams typically would charter themselves to map the current-state process, identify waste in the process, and then "redesign" the process or service line by eliminating or reducing as much of the waste as possible. VSM teams typically spanned multiple departments and involved many functional areas and staff. Large-scale VSM projects expose the biggest gaps and wastes in the process and result in many smaller Lean projects that span from Kaizen events to focused A3 projects. The hope with large VSM teams is to start getting the organization to see and eliminate the waste across the value stream and working in a more process-centered way to improve the organization. The challenge with most VSM implementations

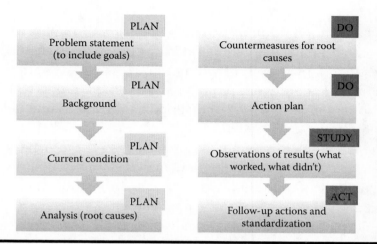

Figure 7.1   Picture of the A3 problem-solving process.

is the time it takes to implement a complete VSM (sometimes could take up to 1 year) and the dramatic amount of change involved for staff and leaders. The other challenge with traditional VSM implementations was keeping the VSM team focused on their "process" goals while still trying to manage their departmental demands and goals. Staff often felt torn between their unit/departmental duties and the "VSM-team" duties and goals and over time this extra work, stress, and conflict pushed many staff and healthcare leaders to simply "give up" on their VSM goals and fall back on their unit goals/duties.

LDM goes to where staff and leaders are at; it doesn't force them into a process-centered organization until they are ready for that kind of radical shift. Implementing LDM around key value streams or service lines gives leaders and staff an intermediate step from purely silo'ed goal setting and work to process goal setting and work. As leaders round across value streams or service lines, there will be a natural alignment. Leaders will start to see problems that upstream LDM boards are having and how it affects the downstream LDM boards. Leaders can prioritize escalated ideas or A3 projects based on the relative importance to the service line or process.

The VSM process is still a very important Lean tool to understand how the patient flows through our key service lines/processes and understanding where waste may be, improved flow may be needed, and so on; however, when coupled with an LDM system it becomes manageable and sustainable and continues to improve on a daily rhythm.

Staff will also start to pull Lean standard work projects/efforts to create stability and consistency in their work. Some may ask why, what do you mean by a standard work project? Why wouldn't you simply just create the standard work and implement it? Standard work certainly should not be a complicated thing; however, staff will not know where to start with standardization and standard work so some just-in-time training will be needed along with some initial coaching and support to help the unit get their standard work in place.

Much like A3 problem solving and projects, we recommend the Lean coach/Lean office train and develop key managers on standard work so they can support their staff with this Lean tool as their staff begins to pull it in.

Once again standard work isn't the goal in itself, it's used as a method/tool by leaders and staff to achieve and sustain their LDM goals; every Lean tool is pulled and used as appropriate by leaders and staff to achieve their LDM goals.

Leaders and staff don't feel pressured to complete standard work or an A3 or any other Lean tool as part of a centralized "Lean training and development" mandate. There's a natural pull for the Lean tools as leaders and staff need them.

Leveraging Key Managers that have a Natural Talent for Lean Projects and LDM

As you develop and implement LDM and Lean projects, you will find that some leaders will have a natural talent for building and managing their LDM board, conducting leader rounds, leader daily disciplines, and Lean projects. It will be key for you to leverage these leaders to help the Lean office/Lean coach deploy LDM and Lean projects across the organization.

Leaders who have a natural talent for LDM and Lean projects should be identified early on. Senior leadership along with the Lean office/coach should be developing these leaders for bigger roles and time to allow them to help other units as part of their development.

As mentioned earlier, Lean projects need to tie back to LDM board goals. A3, 5S, standard work, and other Lean tools and projects can be displayed in the diagnosis (analysis) section and treatment plan sections of the LDM board so staff can easily make the connection to the Lean project and their LDM board. Making Lean projects visible on the LDM board ensures staff are also making progress toward their implementation "treatment" plan.

Lean projects will still require the executive sponsor, team, and Lean coach to set aside time to more deeply understand, analyze, and develop action plans for the more difficult problems; however, the amount of time to follow up on action plans and sustainment efforts is dramatically reduced with LDM. Daily rounding ensures that project action plans are moving forward and progress on previously implemented Lean projects are not sliding back. Lean implementation and the movement of the LDM board goals in the right direction remain the focus and the project team can see progress week to week on their LDM boards.

Kaizen events (rapid improvement efforts) are another Lean tool that many organizations have led Lean transformations with traditionally. Kaizen events take a small area or unit and using a rapid "plan–do–study–act (PDSA)" methodology, implement dramatic change in a week or so. Kaizen events are very effective at building the organization's ability to implement change quickly and engage staff and leaders alike. Each day of the week-long Kaizen event is designed to quickly uncover waste and implement Lean tools to address the waste. By the end of the week, historically the Kaizen team would build a "report out" presentation and celebrate their successes. LDM gives the Kaizen team a daily "scoreboard" to more effectively show progress and highlight where the team needs help without disrupting staff or leaders, it's built right into the process!

Project management isn't traditionally a skill that many healthcare organizations are very good at. LDM creates a management process that drives daily execution and gets staff in the habit of implementing ideas as they pertain to their LDM board goals. The pull for project management from frontline staff and leaders, much like Lean tools, becomes a natural thing. Project management isn't typically a skill set that most healthcare managers are very strong with as they struggle to keep up with the plethora of other duties and tasks to manage their business (including driving LDM).

Healthcare managers can and should certainly learn to use basic Lean tools and methods in support of their LDM board and system; however, it may be more helpful to have bigger projects managed by professional project managers. Lean coaches are trained to run Lean projects and can train a small cadre of Lean project managers to lead the numerous Lean projects that will require a trained and skillful project manager. The notion that middle managers can learn all the Lean tools, develop into skilled project managers, and still manage their business is simply unrealistic. From my experience, loading too much upon the shoulders of middle managers too fast is a recipe for frustration, alienation, and dissatisfaction within the middle management ranks.

Middle managers early on will need lots of coaching and help to implement their LDM system. As simple Lean projects emerge, they can (with the assistance of a Lean coach) manage smaller Lean A3 projects or standard work projects. For more difficult Lean projects that require greater knowledge of the Lean tools and methods and advanced facilitation, bringing in a trained and experienced project manager from the Lean office will save staff and the middle managers lots of unnecessary frustration.

Remember, Lean needs to be a pull not a push! Pushing more tools and methods onto staff and leadership than they are ready will create resentment and unnecessary frustration. One of the powerful effects of LDM is the way it drives senior leadership to either resource the toughest, systematic issues and ideas that are escalating from front-line LDM boards or scope the issue down in a way that allows for a smaller, simpler solution that might not resolve the entire issue, but address the most affected front-line units. A good rule of thumb for improvement is for 80% of the improvement actions to occur between your front-line LDM boards and the director level LDM boards. In most healthcare organizations, 80% of the improvement is coming as a push from middle management and senior leadership, which means a lot more large-scale projects that require more skilled project managers, much more change-management to implement and gain buy-in from staff and constant "pushing" from senior leadership upon the organization. Using LDM to engage middle managers and front-line staff to problem solve and improve 80% of the issues that arise day to day will become your organization's greatest strength and asset; the ability of your staff and mid-level leaders to execute their goals daily and innovate and improve performance using fundamental Lean methods. This is the real "magic" of Toyota, developing staff and leaders to drive improvement daily.

Too many Lean implementations blindly start off with enterprise-wide Lean projects that have very large project scopes and teams and take a huge amount of time and energy to implement. LDM enables many smaller Lean projects to focus on those front-line LDM boards that truly have the greatest need. Failed large-scale change projects have a lasting effect on staff and leaders. LDM is very much the incremental approach to change within the organization. Senior staff can rattle off the last 5 or 10 large-scale project failures over the last 5–10 years. Leadership's credibility is on the line.

Larger scope Lean projects also take a much more experienced and senior (usually higher salaried) project manager, hence another reason to keep most of your Lean project as small as possible by scoping them down first and then deploying them across the organization.

Most directors and middle managers (and some front-line staff) can be developed to manage small A3 projects as mentioned earlier. Establishing regular A3 workshops whereby the attendee must bring a real problem from their LDM board and work on that during the workshop and follow on coaching can do two things:

1. Trains and develops leaders and staff in the A3 problem-solving process (and gets them comfortable managing these small focused Lean projects).
2. Launches several A3 projects to address real LDM board action-items/ issues. Leaders and staff learn by doing with real data and info from their LDM board.

The Lean office and Lean sensei's first and foremost job is to build the LDM system (leadership rounds, leader daily disciplines, and LDM boards). As LDM matures, Lean projects will quickly escalate to leaders who will then look to the Lean office to support Lean projects to address them. A3 problem-solving, coaching, and training (with real escalated problems from LDM boards) in a workshop style setting as discussed earlier will allow the Lean office to skill up key leaders who can then run-start to launch their own A3s. Keeping most of the Lean projects scoped down to the A3 level as possible early on allows the Lean office to develop and leverage as many leaders as possible to address the early demand for small-scale Lean project support.

As larger more complex Lean projects surface, the Lean office will need to resource and lead these. The challenge will be supporting the ongoing A3 training, coaching, and development of leaders to support the vast majority of small-scale Lean projects and problem solving that LDM will create the ongoing support and development of the LDM system and finally support key large-scale Lean projects. Each of your Lean team will have varying levels of Lean project management, coaching, and training skills so expecting each of them to juggle a little bit of each of these may be a little unrealistic at first. Everyone on the Lean team should be supporting the development of LDM within the organization as this is the primary first step for any Lean transformation. Training, coaching, and developing leaders to run small-scale A3 problem-solving projects is something that most junior-level Lean team members can do relatively quickly and easily.

Large-scale, complex, enterprise-wide Lean projects should be reserved for your most senior Lean team members. These projects require the most facilitation, change management, and highest level of project management.

As junior Lean team members grow in their practice, they must eventually learn to lead the larger, tougher Lean projects.

It will be a challenge to keep as many of your Lean projects as small and focused as possible. Leaders have come to expect big projects as a solution to big problems, but the truth is that the reverse is true. Small projects (many of them) are truly the solution to big problems, why? Smaller focused projects go through the PDSA process much faster. Leaders and staff can digest the changes much easier and faster. Small projects oftentimes don't require large teams (less resources) and don't require as much structure (simply A3 form will do most of the time). Deployment of successful small projects with quantifiable results can be as easy as sharing the successful A3 form (with action plan) with other units with a similar problem.

Without LDM small projects don't make as much sense, because the organization cannot share and transfer successful action plans very easily (there really isn't a mechanism to do that well). Leadership rounds create a mechanism for successful small Lean projects to spread across the organization. Leaders communicate and connect their departmental units with successful A3s in other parts of their department that may not normally communicate with each other. Leaders also communicate and share A3s from other departments and other sites they learn about from their LDM reviews with senior leadership. Front-line units start pulling A3s from other units that have successfully tackled similar problems and learning and improvement accelerate.

LDM gives Lean projects and methods a solid foundation to "stick" to. Advanced Lean tools (including Six Sigma tools and methods), Lean layout/design (cell design), single-piece flow, mistake proofing, statistical process analysis, and start to make more sense to leaders and staff once LDM is in place and a certain amount of problem solving using foundational Lean tools has occurred. Lean foundational tools include 5S, standard work, visual management, A3 problem solving, and root cause analysis primarily.

Fundamental PDSA problem-solving cycles gradually transition to foundational Lean tool use, which gradually transitions to advanced Lean Six Sigma tool use. Not all leaders and staff in the organization will need or use Lean advanced tools so it's important to make sure you focus on those leaders and staff that have a solid grasp on LDM and foundational Lean use first. It's better to spend more time with foundational tools and get staff solid on A3 problem solving, for example, than to move too fast toward advanced Lean tools.

When implementing advanced Lean tools, as with LDM, it's a good idea to develop "model lines" or key areas that have truly mastered that particular tool and can "show" the rest of the organization what a Lean "cell," single-piece flow, or 3P Lean layout looks like.

Lean layout is especially useful when the organization is looking at new construction. The layout of a department or hospital has a profound impact on staff and patient flow, communication, and the overall patient experience. Lean layout starts with the existing blueprints or layouts of a department or hospital and examines (with cross-functional staff involved in the key processes within that department) seven key flows:

Patient-flow: This is the primary flow that all other flows attempt to optimize.

Physician/Provider-flow: Ideally we want to keep providers as close to their exam and procedure rooms as possible while still giving them a quiet space to work on administrative tasks.

Nurse-flow: Nurses typically walk 3 miles per day because of poor layout. Nursing station location and design as well as supply and equipment room locations and design can reduce wasteful motion for nurses by as much as 30%.

Support staff-flow (Techs, front desk staff, etc.): Design and location of the front desk, location of patient and staff restrooms are keys to communication and allowing front and back office staff to help each other during peak times.

Equipment-flow: Location and design of support equipment within the department can not only reduce wasted motion, but minimize the "hunt and seeking" of equipment across the department.

Supply-flow: A large amount of wasted time is spent walking to supply rooms and looking for the right supplies within the supply area. Thoughtful location and design of supply areas will not only reduce wasted time, but also help control inventory levels and waste that tend to get "stashed" across the department.

Flow of clean/dirty linens: The flow of clean and dirty linens is called out because it often is something that gets overlooked. Linen management is no small thing for many hospitals, so it's important to optimize linen storage and flow as well.

Lean layout initially starts with quick "just-in-time" Lean training (Lean wastes, understanding flow) and then moves into a review of the blueprints or layout of the department or area impacted. Identifying the cross-functional team is key. Make sure to include support groups such as maintenance and house-keeping staff. Using seven different colored yarn and pushpins to represent the different flows, Lean coaches facilitate the team through each flow using the current-state layout. As the team walks through each flow, the bottlenecks and design flaws will be clear to all (look for long stretches of yarn, back and forth, or yarn that is stretched all over the place versus tight yarn circles or paths).

As you identify these design issues, write them down on yellow stickie notes on the current-state layout alongside the yarn. Tape everything down really well; as this layout will travel from time to time and everything will tend to fall off. Take pictures of your current-state layout with the yellow stickie note issues.

Using the current-state blueprint with yarn and stickies have the team cut out the rooms and key areas from a copy of the original blueprint so the team can move rooms and key areas around. Starting with the patient-flow start to walk thru the layout, letting the team try different options for loca-tions of rooms and key areas. After the team has developed several design "iterations" and has come to a final design they like best, remove the yarn from the finished layout and compare it to the yarn from the initial blueprint to learn how much improvement is made with respect to motion. Be sure to also capture savings from areas and rooms that the team was able to elimi-nate or save or reduce. Document your overall linear feet savings for each flow from the yarn before and after as well as the overall square footage savings the team has achieved by eliminating wasteful use of space. To gain buy-in form the rest of the department and key stakeholders, find a spot where staff can come in and see the before and after with your savings and allow them a chance to offer feedback on a separate board or sheet.

Batch reduction and moving toward single piece flow in the hospital is no small achievement and should be reserved for leaders and teams that have already achieved significant Lean foundational improvements such as standard work, 5S, and visual management. Batch reduction in the blood lab is a great place to start if the team and leaders are ready. Mapping the flow of blood samples from blood draw to the lab and then to the provider will highlight "batching" of samples almost every step of the way. Depending on how big the batch is it's often a good experiment to try and reduce the batch by a third to see how much stress that puts on the system versus how much benefit we get in the way of cycle time and reduced hemolyzed samples.

Batching occurs for many reasons. Batching can occur due to geography; in other words if someone has to take a blood sample 500 feet away, they will be inclined to wait until they have a sufficient number of samples and then transport them over in a "batch" to reduce the number of trips they have to make and essentially optimize their time at the expense of the process.

Another example of batching occurs when a machine is set up to run a certain number of items all together (it's essentially built into the process). An example of this is the centrifuge in the lab. Just because we have 25 slots doesn't mean we have to wait to use all 25; however, our instincts will be to wait until we have 25 to be efficient with respect to the machine once again at the expense of the process. Simply cutting the batch once again by a third (using roughly 17 of the slots in the centrifuge) the team can experiment with the stress placed on the system versus the benefit in cycle time (the reduced time savings will allow providers to get lab results sooner and get back with anxious patients sooner regarding their blood work). Since blood work is so commonly used throughout the hospital, a cycle time improvement in the lab can have a huge impact across many departments throughout the hospital.

Lean cell design and Lean layout go hand in hand; however, sometimes Lean cells can be created without any significant construction. Lean cells follow the flow of the patient or product (blood sample, X-ray, MRI, etc.). As with Lean layout, you want to work with teams that have already successfully used Lean foundational tools such 5S, standard work, and visual management. Some just-in-time Lean training will help prepare the team for the Lean cell design exercise (Lean wastes and flow). Starting with the existing layout, have the team map out the current flow capturing key measures along the way such as process times, wait times between process steps, first-time quality through each process step. Capturing the current state is key because it gives the team a baseline for improvement as well helps them visualize how broken their existing flow is and where. Creating a Lean cell requires Lean foundational tools such as standard work, flow, balanced work, and waste reduction used together to create either a U-shaped, L-shaped, or I-shaped cell. The goal of the cell isn't just to rearrange furniture so everyone's lined up like a process. The goal of the Lean cell is to create flow and make breakdowns more visible so team members can better help each other out. If all we do is rearrange chairs and don't address the waste, flow, use visual management to trigger and communicate more effectively and implement standard work with balanced work built in, then we wind up with the same delays and bottlenecks as before in a tighter space!

Lean cells require that team members understand the "fringes" of each other's work so they can help upstream or downstream as issues occur. Lean cells create a natural "cross-training" within the cell as the closer proximity and standard work allows team members to cover for each other more and more. As Lean cells mature, it is natural to see two positions merge into one as waste is removed. Lean cells that started off with 10 team members can oftentimes be reduced to seven or six team members over time while improving cycle time, quality and patient satisfaction. As with other advanced Lean tools, it's best to create a "model Lean cell" for others to learn from first. Lean cells that are rushed and "pushed" from senior leadership often result in frustrated staff and unhappy patients. Lean cells take time and you cannot skip Lean foundational tools.

Mistake proofing or "poka-yoke" is another advanced Lean tool that is often used in conjunction with development of standard work. Teams that are developing standard work are trying to gain consistency in their work processes; however, quality and safety must be built in as well. Mistake proofing takes many forms. Start-up checklists are the most basic forms of mistake proofing. Color coding is used to make errors more visible as well. Mechanical mistake proofing involves designing fittings and connections that only work with the correct match. The idea of mistake proofing isn't necessarily to design one perfect design, but to pull together a variety of mistake proofing designs to dramatically reduce the probability of an error or failure. An example of this is designing a start-up checklist, coupled with visual pictures of the right and the wrong way to do a job, coupled with a mechanical "no go" gage to check the finished product.

As front-line units gain understanding and familiarity with tracking and managing their LDM boards, using Six Sigma tools and methods can be introduced to help understand the data from their run-chart (symptoms) and diagnosis (analysis) a little deeper. Statistical analysis tools such as histograms/distribution analysis, Pareto analysis, process capability, and others can be introduced. Lean tools and methods are the "building blocks" for process management that get staff engaged in their metrics and data with relatively easy to learn and understand tools and methods. Six Sigma tools and methods come into play after teams have reached a certain level of sophistication and comfort with their data. Remember the idea is to embed these tools and methods within the organization, not to have it held by just a few highly skilled experts.

Chapter 8

Integrating LDM and "Competing" Complementary Initiatives

Throughout this field guide, we have been talking about implementing an active, meaningful, and "living" Lean daily management (LDM) system, including rounding, LDM boards, problem solving, improving metrics, and other meaningful aspects of deployment.

At this point, it is critical to discuss a very pragmatic aspect of successfully (and sustainably!) building a meaningful LDM program that this sort of initiative is rarely done in a "vacuum" without other competing and/or overlapping initiatives! For example, most hospitals and healthcare organizations have quality, cost-reduction, service excellence, patient safety, compliance, electronic mail record (EMR) and other system implementations, department-specific initiatives, documentation improvement initiatives, patient-flow, education, training, and so on.

The amount of change that these multiple initiatives represent is absolutely astounding and overwhelming for most of the hospital staff! Add to this, a fundamentally different way of managing an organization through LDM boards can seem like "the last straw" and cause many of the staff to think that "this too shall pass" and simply try and do the minimum. They may see LDM boards as being "just one more thing" in a sea of countless initiatives. We can't let this take hold of the critical work of building our LDM system! LDM boards are not "just one more thing," but rather a flexible and dynamic tool and approach that can fundamentally change the functioning of the overall organization and help these other initiatives succeed! Therefore, LDM is not just another competing initiative, but an "enabler" for the other efforts.

Another perspective to help illustrate this is the growing body of knowledge and research that shows how habits drive most individuals and organizations in very fundamental ways. When an individual is doing something that is habitual, brain patterns illustrate that the beginning and end of the task are very active mentally, but the times in-between are basically on "autopilot." Therefore, when a habit is hardwired, there is little conscious thought going on; it is "the way we do things around here," which is also one of the best definitions of organizational culture! Culture is fundamentally the things that we as individuals, and as an organization, do naturally and without much intentional thought or effort.

When an individual (or extrapolating the concept to an organization as a "big brain," which isn't too much of a leap in logic!) is learning a new skill or approach, he or she is "fighting the natural drive to follow the old habit" and do things in a different way. Brain patterns show much more activity between the beginning and end of the activity or task, showing that the brain is working hard to be much more conscious about every aspect of the task. This mental load is taking a lot more mental effort than the old "habit." This additional effort creates a real incentive for the individual (or the organization) to drift back to the old habit. It is just easier and requires less mental effort! The process of turning a new task or skill into a habit takes time—the more "cycles of learning" or doing the new task or activity, the less mental activity it takes, and the more it is a "habit" than a "new thing." The rule of thumb is that it takes 30 days for a new habit to be formed, so if we try something new and don't keep it up for a sufficient period of time, then we are going to drift back to where we started!

The discussion thus far has been related to trying "one thing" differently and changing one habit. Now, take a moment to think about all of the potential (and common) competing change-initiatives that are likely "on the plate" of a floor-nurse or other healthcare staff member! There are potentially dozens of habits or behaviors that are trying to be changed at any one time! This brings to mind the challenge of cognitive overload; the average individual can only handle or manage so much change at one time, and this applies to organizations as well! Each of these competing change initiatives has a variety of different habits or behaviors that need to be changed, which "in a vacuum" would be manageable. When you add it to the other initiatives, each with their seemingly "manageable" number of changes, the total amount of change becomes unmanageable!

This helps explain a common struggle in hospitals and healthcare organizations. Each product, service, initiative, or other undertaking has a proven potential impact, weather it is decreasing patient or staff injuries, improving patient satisfaction, reducing cost or improving some other measure of organizational performance. These metrics are what is used to sell a product or service, and the expectation is that these will be realized. This is especially prevalent with software or technology, with the assumption that they will be used to a significant proportion of their true potential. Hospital executives have become very cynical about these promises, as the results are rarely realized or come anywhere close to being realized!

The problem is not with the technology, or the competing initiative; it is due to the inability of the organization to effectively limit the cognitive overload on the staff (who are also having to do their core jobs and/or provide patient care while trying to adapt to so much change including changing so many habits!). The technology or new initiative is in place, but the inertia of habits and culture (remember, culture is "the way we do things around here") means that the impact of the initiatives or new technology is muted by the lack of a system for managing the change or decreasing the complexity and/or confusion that comes with so much change taking place! The organization is demanding so much of staff and there is so much complexity and change already inherent in a healthcare organization that leaders don't really know exactly what is going on or have the bandwidth or resources to track or hold staff accountable for the change. Staff wind up doing what any rational individual would do in this situation and default back to what they know, their old habits!

So, with such a daunting task what are we to do? Fortunately, there are some very tangible actions that we can take to help with these monumental challenges that all healthcare organizations face!

The first one of these is to not treat the LDM boards as "just one more thing" that is competing with the others. We can instead leverage LDM as a central problem-solving and daily management approach to help support and integrate all of the competing initiatives! If we have a quality challenge with falls and other patient safety issues, we can tackle these at our daily LDM problem-solving sessions instead of them being "quality's problem" or our manager's problem. If we are implementing a service-excellence initiative and working to decrease call lights, improve responsiveness to patients, or another issue, and these involve establishing a new habit or using new scripting, these can be the focus of an LDM board metric! If we are deploying a new EMR, we can avoid the natural response of saying that "we don't have time to do LDM . . . we are implementing an EMR!" and instead restructure/refocus the LDM boards to help capture, analyze, and manage the huge amount of change that is coming from the new EMR deployment. Therefore, the LDM boards are not just another competing initiative that stands alone; it becomes the "glue" or "structure" to hold the other initiatives together and as a mechanism to control the issue of "cognitive overload." There are only a handful of things that staff will focus on at a time and LDM helps them focus on one topic per LDM problem-solving session, so it works naturally for addressing "cognitive overload!"

Some leaders may say "we don't have time to limit the amount of change . . . we need to do all of these things at once . . . and do them now!" While this is understandable given the pressures placed on hospital and healthcare executives and on the organizations in general, the reality is that "hope is not a plan!" Simply mandating or assuming that "they will figure out a way" just doesn't work, and the gap between potential and realized impact of the different initiatives and products grows wider. The frustration and cognitive overload of staff gets more extreme and executives at the organization get increasingly frustrated with staff and with the vendors who promised so much more impact.

As mentioned before, one method for limiting this "cognitive overload" is through the LDM boards and problem solving. Even with LDM, there is still an issue with too many new "things" staff are being asked to do. For example, service excellence, quality, patient flow, LDM, and other initiatives regularly require rounding in specific ways, at specific times, filling out forms and gathering information, meeting with leaders, changing scripting, the list goes on. Staff get overwhelmed by all the "new" things, and see them all as just barriers to providing patient care or doing their jobs and either allow them to fall to the wayside or just fill out the forms and have the meetings, without any real substance.

But what is a leader to do to decrease this complexity? Is there any way forward? Fortunately, there is! It will require some serious thought, collaboration, and discipline, but it will yield significant and long-term benefits if you "stay the course!"

The next step forward for integration of multiple initiatives is rarely undertaken by most organizations primarily due to the following reasons:

1. One of these is that every organization has its own unique combination of "activities" and "things" that it is doing, so integration of these is not "cookie-cutter" but takes focused thought and deliberate effort, which is

not easy. The organization might lack individuals who have the confidence or knowledge to effectively undertake integration and they might be lacking the executive sponsorship to do it effectively (an initiative such as this likely crosses many "silos," so a top-level leader who is above this territoriality will be critical, so that these initiatives are not competing for individual success, but looking to integrate efforts effectively for the overall good of the organization).

2. Another reason is a common phenomenon of "the emperor has no clothes" (*The Emperor's New Clothes,* Tale by Hans Christian Andersen), that is, the senior leaders are not aware that there is a gap between the "things that we should be doing" and the "things we are actually doing." This can be due to either fear of staff and mid-level leaders to make their top leader aware of this gap (which could imply failure and the wrong leadership approach would be to start blaming and accusing the seemingly responsible parties for this common organizational problem of cognitive overload that is not their fault) or a lack of true and meaningful leader rounding and "going to the Gemba" to see firsthand the connection (or lack thereof) between what should be happening and what is happening.

3. The third (and potentially least obvious, but ironically most explainable and also the most easy to address with strong leadership support) is that the consultants working on these competing initiatives or approaches likely have a significant amount of pride, financial incentive, or other considerations (or apparent methodologies or justifications) that they use to "defend their territory." By having their initiatives "discrete," they can defend or justify their results or impacts, justify their existence or budgeting and their professional reputation. Ironically, while these justifications for territory are understandable, their long-term existence almost guarantees these approaches will not be truly integrated or truly "get into the DNA" of the organization. They are just "things" or "activities" that individuals within the organization do (or don't do, which is more common) to "mimic" what they are told to do, without really understanding why or believing what they are doing. Therefore, initiatives remaining in this state are competing and each of them limit the success of the other as individuals and the organization can only handle so much change or "new things/behaviors" at any one time. Many of these vendors focus research and "white papers" on justifying why their approach or initiative needs to "stand alone" and that integration will diminish the effectiveness of their particular "fiefdom." What is

critical to understand is that we are focused on the success and impact of ALL of these initiatives on the WHOLE organization, which will be minimized if these initiatives are left in a state of competition. These initiatives must be simplified and reconciled to close the gap between "what we are supposed to be doing" and "what we are actually doing." In addition, recognizing the reality that all of these competing initiatives or programs exist in an interdependent organization, and the macro/cumulative cognitive load that it causes for staff. Therefore, simplifying and consolidating the competing initiatives is critical for actual realized success.

Let's explore one more relevant consideration before jumping into "how" to effectively integrate these initiatives. When an individual (or an organization) is first beginning to learn a new skill, they need to understand the principles, the "why behind the what," and then have different new "habits" to replicate and practice. The prescriptive approach of many new initiatives or programs is critical early on in the learning process, and could not be successful without it. The challenge is that for organizations to truly develop and deeply integrate and "own" a concept or approach and have it "get into their DNA," they need to move beyond replicating, and begin experimenting and innovating so that the initiative "gets into their DNA" and becomes a living/breathing part of the organization that is dynamic and able to adapt and integrate with the constantly changing organization. Therefore, the concept of integrating multiple competing programs or initiatives needs to take into consideration the comparative maturity of these programs, allowing early initiatives to grow and develop through the "replication" phase and then reach a state where they can be integrated into "your organization's" way! Rather than your organization's culture being a concoction of replicating consultants or other's approaches, they are integrated into a visual, well-thought through, active, and dynamic (living and breathing) part of your organization! If your organization embraces this approach, it will be critical to have new approaches and programs have this as part of their "flight plan." This is progress from replication/repetition to integration into "your organization's" way! The mandate for integration and simplification can (with likely pushback and efforts to dissuade you) be integrated into consulting or other contracts to minimize increased complexity as new initiatives are undertaken. This helps to encourage meaningful development of the organization's understanding about "why we are doing this" and instilling the Lean/Toyota production system (TPS) concept of "long term thinking" into your organization's consulting and/or organizational development programs and investments.

Now that we have that "condition" out of the way and understood, we can delve into the "how" of integration of multiple competing initiatives can be undertaken. This initiative is the deliberate and structured step after utilizing the LDM boards for controlling cognitive overload and beyond just "managing the complexity" to "reducing the complexity!"

As with most Lean/TPS approaches, this integration activity is low-tech, cheap, and heavily utilizes the creativity and brilliance of your staff and the incredible power and approachability of visual management! Also, it is relatively intuitive and straightforward (at least the first part) and can be very inspirational and help instill organizational pride and ownership when done correctly.

The first step is to do an "inventory" of all of the "tasks, activities, things, initiatives, and so on" that are going on in the organization. The initial step to enable this is to set up a meeting (or a series of meetings) with representatives from these different organizational initiatives to represent their particular efforts. At this point, we would recommend NOT including the consultants or external entities that are the initiators of these programs. The reason behind this is that their "paradigm" is potentially so set that they wouldn't be open to this sort of undertaking, and would be incentivized to derail this sort of integrative undertaking. Also, the traditional consulting personality might be so overpowering that they would drown out the voice of the staff. The critical voices for this integrative initiative would be the internal owners who understand the mechanics of the initiatives, the reality of what is happening "on the ground" on the units and elsewhere. These folks also have a greater loyalty to the organization than to the program or initiative.

Once this team is assembled, they can begin listing the "things/activities/tasks" that these competing initiatives are demanding of the staff. This would include scripting, rounding, safety, evaluations, goal setting, metrics, and so on. Each of these activities needs to be written on its own discrete post-it note. The end-goal of this first step is to identify natural groupings of similar, competing, overlapping, or related activities or tasks to identify opportunities for consolidating, distilling, or otherwise simplifying the overly complicated and overwhelming system that "evolved" rather than being "designed." This activity is meant to "design" or "engineer" an integrated and meaningful approach for your organization's improvement and experience initiatives.

As these natural groupings of similar activities begin to appear and grow, a multitude of discussions will begin to arise around "what is that group?, how do they relate?, this one goes in both or between the two?" and similar insights are very healthy discussions and questions! They show that you are yet again harnessing the knowledge, creativity, and brilliance of your staff and organization!

As these groupings continue to develop, questions of adjacencies will then develop, such as "this group feels like it belongs next to that group?" or "these groups overlap," which is again very healthy! Now our understanding of the organization's initiatives (and the initial development of "our organization's" way) has begun! Visually, you are beginning to see a collection of "random post-it notes" developing into a visual structure of similarities, differences, adjacencies, overlaps, and other relationships (see Figure 8.1).

To take a step back at this point is helpful. Imagine you take all of the post-it notes from all of the competing initiatives and scatter them across the wall. Now, bring a staff member in and try to explain it to them. This would be an EXTREMELY PAINFUL undertaking, because you would have to explain each of them by themselves, answer many questions about

Figure 8.1   GRMC picture of integrated map of competing initiatives.

overlap and reconcile them with others (which are GREAT questions!). This is a thought experiment that helps to illustrate why an undertaking to integrate competing initiatives is absolutely critical as otherwise staff just see the "shotgunning" of changes and initiatives throughout the organizations.

Now, imagine that you bring the same staff member in after going through the visual management exercise of grouping similarities, moving groups relative to each other, describing what the groups are, and then consolidating/combining these. How much easier would it be to walk a staff member through this, and how much more confidence would they have in the organization and its vision and management? The investment of thought and planning is readily apparent in the "before" and "after" condition of these post-it notes.

Now, the next step after this grouping of post-it notes and then the adjacencies and relationships of the groups is to begin to describe what we did intuitively in the previous exercise. For example, if a group is a collection of competing rounding initiatives and "rounding-like" activities, then we need to name and describe this group and ask a very fundamental question at a higher level than any of the individual initiatives or programs would ask: "why are we rounding, why is this valuable to the organization, and how can our staff keep these 5 or 10 different 'flavors' of rounding straight and keep them meaningful?" This is asking the "why" behind the "what." With this question being answered we can begin looking for opportunities to consolidate and simplify the rounding systems. For example, there is usually a lot of overlap between the rounding questions that are required, so one might start to wonder if we could combine them to ask simplified and reconciled questions to achieve the fundamental objectives of each! This would involve going through the detailed rounding forms and processes, including frequency and who is doing what, and consolidate them. This takes some work, but the ensuing simplicity is rather profound!

Once we have gone through this process of listing activities, grouping them, arranging and overlapping related groups, and naming them, and then we are at a point where we have a much better understanding of the "why" behind the "what." As leaders, we now have a much better understanding of the "why" and can explain the context much more clearly to our staff.

With this foundation in place, we now proceed to formalizing the natural groupings and consolidations into a model and graphic. This model/graphic is a powerful tool for learning, teaching, and change, which Toyota has demonstrated over the years with its "Toyota house" model. It provides a simple, powerful, and effective graphical representation of "their" system;

staff, leaders, and others can point to this one unifying vision to help provide context and direction to what they are doing and why.

When new staff joins the organization, or there is a presentation to the Board of Directors, this graphical representation of "our way" clearly shows the deep thought, commitment, and efforts to proactively design a system for your healthcare organization. This integrated model (Figure 8.2) clearly shows how to effectively problem solve, develop staff and leaders, align efforts from the strategic plan to the front lines, and prioritize and integrate new initiatives into a meaningful context that provides the "why" behind the "what," which is rare for most organizations.

With the completion of this clearly defined model of "our way" and integrated, streamlined, and consolidated forms, activities, and initiatives, it will be critical to circle back and figure out how to continually align these with the organization. Thinking back to the "current state" that existed

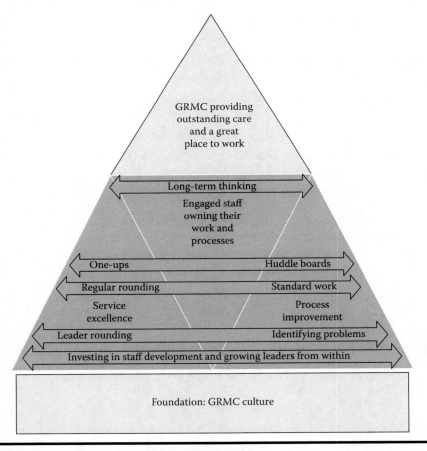

Figure 8.2 Integrated model of competing initiatives.

before this integration, there was a fragmented, overlapping, confusing, and overwhelming list of competing initiatives. In addition, many of these initiatives were struggling to maintain even a rudimentary level of maintenance of associated process discipline after their initial "push" and many had regressed close to their initial pre-implementation state. Now, add to this a seemingly "new" integrated system with similar and related, but different (consolidated and simpler) system, and many staff will think "here we go again . . . more change! More to focus on in addition to just trying to survive the day."

This new integrated initiative will therefore have some "hurdles" to overcome the damage from excessive complexity, cognitive overload, a lack of an LDM board to manage cognitive overload, and seemingly overlapping initiatives have left a lot of frustrated, confused, and apathetic staff.

To overcome this, there will need to be a thoughtful "relaunch" of your organization's "way" not focusing on the negatives, but rather focusing on the gains that have been (or were previously achieved), the potential impact, and the excitement and potential of our new unified, simplified, and more meaningful "way."

To avoid succumbing to the old adage of "those who refuse to learn from the past are doomed to repeat it," it is critical to think carefully about the cognitive overload and confusion/complexity of the multiple competing initiatives that lead to this situation in the beginning! As we are working on "relaunching" aspects of many of these initiatives in a new unified way, we must make sure to do so in a thoughtful, considerate, and meaningful way to avoid repeating the mistakes that got us here! Fortunately, we now have the LDM boards in place as an active and dynamic tool to work through the problems and challenges, as well as limit cognitive overload on our staff by introducing too much change at once (by having our staff focus more on consistent quality of problem solving and change, rather than quantity).

We will need to develop a "flight plan" of which aspects of this new unified and simplified/integrated model to reintroduce and "refresh" into the organization. This plan outlines how to align with individual, departmental, and organizational goals, incentives, and evaluations, and how to effectively integrate leader rounding (going to the "Gemba") to reinforce what we are trying to achieve. The flight plan needs to (1) limit the amount of change that is being introduced into the organization at any one time (limiting cognitive overload), (2) support problem solving and integration, (3) allow for sufficient time to ensure that integration and success is achieved before moving on to new changes (focusing on quality rather than quantity of change), and (4) ensure ongoing focus on maintenance and continuous improvement of your new organization's "way" to continue to adapt to your organization's constantly changing environment and challenges. In addition, it should be structured to help keep your organization's "way" fresh and meaningful as the organization's needs, challenges, and opportunities evolve.

By focusing on integration and defining your organization's "way," you are avoiding the trap of "check the box" initiatives where overlapping and competing initiatives limit each other's success. Defining your organization's "way" helps develop an ongoing framework and model to evaluate and incrementally integrate future initiatives and changes. By proactively defining your organization's "way," you are moving toward playing "offense" instead of "defense," and your organization is likely to start innovating and defining new best practices that go above and beyond what external consulting entities are trying to sell to your organization. Your organization's internal problem solving and innovation capacity is likely to increase dramatically. With integration, the amount of resources spent on external "experts" is likely to decrease dramatically, as your internal expertise, knowledge, and experience will exceed those of external entities. Therefore, resources can be expended internally within the organization, developing your staff, and focusing more on proactive problem solving. This is the case at Toyota, where there is a significantly lower rate of expenditure on external consultants and resources, as Toyota already defines world-class manufacturing. The power of your organization defining its own "way" (rather than other organizations defining it for you), developing your own staff and promoting from within, and then proactively innovating and growing your organization through "playing offense" is an exciting prospect and is a stark contrast to the "firefighting" that most organizations are stuck in!

Chapter 9

Identifying a Lean Sensei and Developing Your Lean Team

Much like buying or building a house, getting back into shape or transforming any part of your life, identifying the right person to help you get started is going to be key. Great leaders realize that they need the right people to get any job done. We recommend that any organization looking to bring Lean into their organization take the time to learn the basics of Lean by either buying a few good books or by attending a Lean healthcare workshop (be sure to look for a workshop put on by individuals who have real experience implementing Lean in a real healthcare setting). There are a lot of non-healthcare workshops out there, but the difference is not necessarily going to be the technical Lean concepts, but more the experience of applying Lean methods in a hospital or clinic environment.

Once you have a basic understanding of what Lean is (and is not), it's time to look for a Lean sensei to help build your transformation plan. If you want to know one of the big differences between successful Lean implementations and failed implementations, it comes down to a few things:

1. Lack of C-level (primarily the chief executive officer [CEO]) understanding, buy-in and consistent practice (Lean Daily Management [LDM] not in place or not consistent and effective)
2. Lack of Lean office talent (inability of the Lean coach or Lean office to develop and execute an effective Lean implementation plan to include

coaching and developing LDM with leaders and staff as well as executing successful Lean projects)

3. Lack of an effective Lean sensei

So why is the Lean sensei so important? Let's go back to the earlier example of trying to lose weight without an effective weight-loss coach. Think of the last time you tried to lose 15–20 pounds and how frustrating that was. What did you do to prepare for this change? Did you first study more about nutrition and proper exercise regimes or did you simply read an article in a magazine and follow that? Maybe you asked a good friend about their routine and tried to follow that? How did that work for you?

For most of us, it resulted in a lot of work and frustration only to wind up back where we were originally; the same holds true for Lean transformations. Learning the fundamentals of Lean and LDM gives you enough knowledge to identify the right Lean sensei and Lean team.

Identifying an effective Lean sensei to help gain C-level (and CEO) buy-in as well as build and develop your Lean team will dramatically improve the speed and success at which you can transform your organization.

Listed below are some criteria to use when identifying the right Lean sensei for your organization (Figure 9.1).

It's helpful to have a Lean sensei that is outside the organization because they can give you the honest feedback you and your leadership team will need to hear as they mature. Lean sensei's are natural coaches and

Positives	Negatives
Outside the organization	Part of the current culture and establishment
Actively writing	Minimal activity in the Lean community
Focused on training	Focused on sales
Focused on cultural transformation	Focused on projects
Prove results in the short term	Promise results over the long term
Simplified explanations in plain English	Technical jargon and Japanese terms
Clear exit point	Indefinite commitment
Transformational experience	Project management experience
Associated with a University or other credible organizations	Unaffiliated, independent, self-created methodology
Actively mentoring and coaching previous clients	No connection with previous clients
Asks questions	Gives answers
Simple Lean explanations	Complicated Lean solutions

Figure 9.1 Lean sensei criteria.

teachers and will generally be associated with a credible university or teaching organization. Lean senseis are also passionate about mentoring and coaching Lean. They should be able to give you names of leaders from other organizations they have helped transform in healthcare. They should be actively engaged in their Lean practice (actively coaching or consulting with other healthcare organizations). Finally an effective Lean sensei should have written white papers, conducted research, or written books on Lean transformation.

Some Key Questions You Can Ask (Identifying a Lean Sensei)

Questions to ask:

- Who have you helped most recently?
  - Diversity by title, helping peers, people outside the contract, local universities, mentoring students, assisting former clients
- How many have you coached and trained?
  - Should be over 1000. Follow up with probing questions to verify.
  - 50–100 probably means they have been focused on project work. Organizational change cannot be done with only 50–100 people.
- What type of people have you taught and mentored?
  - Frontline, middle managers, senior leadership, outside normal operations (information technology, human resources [HR]), interns and students, future Lean leaders and champions.
- What environments have you rolled out management systems in?
  - Profit, nonprofit, union, nonunion.
- Where can I see your writing?
- When can I expect you to leave?
- How do I know if you have been successful?
- How do you develop yourself professionally?
  - Community of Lean thinkers, conferences
- Who is/are your senseis?
- What is the next step in your learning?

Establishing a Lean sensei early on will help the Lean team quickly get on the same page and get pointed in the right direction. C-level buy-in is in many ways a function of the ability of the Lean team (and Lean sensei) to train and develop them into Lean leaders and into the cadence of an LDM system. The Lean leader you hire may or may not always be a seasoned or effective "Lean sensei" so having the Lean sensei there early on to help with the development of senior leadership and development of the Lean team will address the two most important pieces of your Lean transformation.

A good Lean sensei should be able to clearly and simply explain what they will do and when they will leave. Lean senseis are there to give start-up support and help develop the senior leadership team and your Lean team primarily. The goal of the sensei is to get the organization to accomplish these two tasks (develop senior leadership and the Lean office) as quickly and effectively as possible. Lean senseis should not be involved in tactical Lean projects unless they are using that project to develop leaders or the Lean team.

Lean senseis are trying to teach leadership and the Lean team to "think" and "act" Lean, which means they are going to ask more questions than give answers. Beware the Lean sensei with all the answers. The Lean sensei will primarily be looking to develop people.

Managing your Lean sensei will be key. Challenge your Lean sensei to develop senior leadership and the Lean team in half the time they recommend. Force them to think outside the box. Don't let your Lean sensei become your boss. Make sure there are clear roles and responsibilities for the Lean sensei and very clear time lines. Manage a Lean sensei to weekly deliverables. Make the Lean sensei clearly state weekly milestones so everyone is clear on what is expected. Senior leadership will want a Lean sensei plan; make sure you get one that has weekly deliverables, milestones, key actions and action owners, and time lines.

Interview your potential Lean sensei candidates. It may be helpful to interview as many as three to four potential Lean sensei candidates to hear their different approaches and to help your senior leadership ascertain which Lean sensei "fits" best with your organization and culture. Beware the senseis that charge for everything. Initial consultation should be free of charge. Some Lean senseis may even offer a free initial assessment, so take advantage of that opportunity.

Make sure your Lean sensei reports to the Lean leader and not the CEO directly. It will become increasingly difficult to manage a Lean sensei if he or she can simply go around your back to the CEO. Identifying and using an effective Lean sensei can dramatically improve the success of your Lean transformation; however you must ensure the Lean sensei is well managed and has a very clear scope of work.

Developing a Lean team in healthcare is more than just making sure everyone is effectively trained and using LDM and Lean methods, but more importantly building an environment of trust and respect within the team. Lean practitioners tend to focus more on the technical pieces of Lean and less on the interpersonal skills that will be needed to effectively coach and develop Lean leaders and staff.

Developing your staff to implement LDM is the first priority. Your Lean sensei can help you with this key piece. Senior Lean coaches will work with C-level leaders to implement LDM and will therefore need greater C-level coaching experience in addition to Lean tools and project experience. Look for senior Lean coaches that are teachers as well as practitioners. Senior coaches will spend as much as 40%–50% of their time teaching, coaching, and developing Lean leaders and staff as well junior Lean coaches. Senior Lean coaches will also need to lead and facilitate higher-level Lean projects.

Junior Lean coaches need to have passion for Lean first and foremost. This may seem obvious, however there are a lot of folks looking to use the Lean office as either a retirement spot or a stepping-stone to another job (the latter isn't necessarily a bad thing as long as leaders practice Lean as they move up in the organization). Your senior and junior Lean coaches need to have passion because they need to energize leaders and staff to stick with LDM and Lean under some very tough circumstances. Junior Lean coaches should have a solid understanding of Lean fundamentals (Lean certification, Lean knowledge, Lean project experience). Coach-ability is important, but initiative is more important. Have your senior Lean coaches help identify, hire, and develop new junior coaches. Every junior coach needs to work with their senior Lean coach to develop a detailed development plan and time line to include Lean fundamentals (LDM basics, 5S, A3 problem solving, standard work, flow, value stream mapping [VSM]), Lean project facilitation and coaching, interpersonal skills, and use of the benefits bank.

The timeline for a junior Lean coach to develop into a senior may take anywhere from 2 to 3 years. Learning LDM and Lean fundamentals is key; however the biggest challenge will be coaching and developing senior leadership. Senior Lean coaches need to expose junior Lean coaches to as many senior leadership coachings and training events as possible.

Junior Lean coaches will need to start with front-line supervisor training and coaching opportunities as part of basic LDM leader development (building LDM boards, leader rounds, leader daily disciplines) and fundamental

Lean Projects (A3 problem solving, Standard Work, 5S, etc.). Over time, the development of their leaders to implement LDM effectively as well as implement Lean projects will be the best evidence that the junior Lean coach is ready to coach and develop more senior leaders. As it turns out, the more effective a junior Lean coach is with developing front-line supervisors the more that department's senior leadership will want to work with that particular junior Lean coach.

The entire Lean team should audit each other's work each week or biweekly if possible. The best learning and development of the team does not come from classroom training on various Lean methods, but from real Lean work done by the team. Everyone gets a chance to share what's working for him or her and what's not working so well. It's important for these Lean audits or walk-throughs to be an opportunity to learn and improve not necessarily critique or criticize. Each week a Lean coach should be prepared to walk the Lean team through some of their work (LDM boards, Lean project work, Lean training events, etc.). At the end of the audit, the team should have a chance to ask "what's worked" and "what's not working" and then give feedback.

This weekly or biweekly review of each Lean team member's work will develop the team more than any classroom or individual training/coaching event. This approach to Lean team development also makes sure that the learning and development is taking place in the context of real Lean work and not in a vacuum. Many Lean teams will get caught up in debates over methods and tools, but the best discussions come from seeing real Lean work and learning from that.

The Lean office leader's personality and behavior sets the environment for learning and development within the Lean team and the Lean transformation. It's important for the Lean office leader to be open to new ideas and interpretations of Lean. Lean coaches can sometimes get so involved in their own work that they are unaware of the initiatives and changes happening around them. It's important for the Lean office leader to keep the team ahead of upcoming organizational changes and to create an environment where Lean coaches can come together and learn from each other. Every Lean coach brings their own unique strengths to the team as well as areas for improvement. The areas for improvement will usually be more obvious and the strengths might be overlooked. Every Lean coach should have the confidence to know that they have the support of any other Lean team member.

Just as any other high performing teams, the Lean team will need time to develop as a team off-site. Organizing off-site team building events that allow team members to learn more about each other in a safe and fun environment will build the much needed trust and help the team know that it's OK to fail, as long as we learn and grow from it. Fear of failure can hold back the Lean team, especially junior Lean coaches.

Establishing a regular dialogue of "things I could have done better" opens the team up to improvement of their own Lean work, as well as learning and growing. Lean coaches tend to learn more from failures than they do from successes. Lean office leaders can become so intensely involved with LDM and Lean transformation that they forget to have fun. Many Lean teams have turnover because the job simply isn't fun anymore. Most Lean office leaders are not the funniest people in the world, so it may be helpful to have someone from outside the team or even outside the organization set up regular fun events. Lean costume contest or Lean joke competitions let the team poke fun at some of the more stressful parts of their jobs in a safe way.

Ultimately one of the most important jobs of the Lean office leader is to develop his or her team. Senior Lean coaches will certainly develop junior Lean coaches; however every Lean team member needs to spend at least 1–2 hours per week learning from the Lean office leader. Some Lean office leaders are appointed to the position because of their leadership skills and experience within the organization and may not have the deep Lean knowledge and experience they may need to develop Lean coaches on the technical pieces of Lean which is actually OK. The Lean leader can either bring in technical Lean training or work with a senior Lean coach who may have deeper Lean technical knowledge. The key here is that the Lean office leader still needs to be engaged in learning and eventually tailoring the technical Lean knowledge to their organization. The Lean sensei can help the Lean office and senior leadership learn the technical pieces of Lean early on and then start to phase out once everyone has a working grasp of the technical pieces of LDM and other Lean methods.

In addition to the technical parts of Lean, the Lean office leader should also focus on developing his or her staff on the softer skills needed to be successful within the organization. Every Lean coach has strengths and weaknesses in their Lean practice and most of the time it's not so much a technical Lean issue but rather soft skill issue.

Key Lean soft skills to develop are as follows:

- "Two ears one mouth" means listen twice as much as you talk.
- "Go see" means that in order to learn we must go to the Gemba first; data are important but must be understood in the context of the workplace.

- *"Multiply yourself"* refers to the Lean coach's ability to not only teach and coach others, but to engage others in a way that allows the Lean coach to support more staff and Lean projects.
- *"People, then process, then technology"* ensures that the Lean coach always starts with the person first and their fears, anxieties, issues, concerns and then moves to the more technical process pieces and finally to any automation or technology pieces; many junior Lean coaches will want to jump straight to technical process issues and most staff will want a quick technology fix.

Many Lean office leaders struggle with whom to hire for junior and senior Lean coaches. Your Lean sensei can certainly help you with identifying the right mix of Lean coaching and practice experience, clinical/healthcare experience, interpersonal skills, teaching experience, and of course overall fit with your team and the organization. Because Lean is still relatively "new" to healthcare (there aren't a lot of truly seasoned Lean healthcare coaches out there), it's probably a good idea to bring in a good mix of folks that can learn and grow from each other. So is it more important to learn healthcare first or learn Lean first?

From personal experience (deploying Lean in manufacturing, energy, banking, insurance, and finally healthcare) the Lean principles don't really change, but the approach and way you engage leaders and staff may change based on the industry and their culture. I have seen too many process improvement programs flounder because they didn't have enough Lean technical knowledge and relied more on clinical experience. The Lean coach is truly the keeper of the Lean methodology and tools not just a really smart clinician who knows all the "best practices" from past experiences. This is not to say that clinical expertise and knowledge isn't key; it absolutely is. However, your site leaders and staff will be looking to your office for Lean methods and tools and not quick answers to what's worked in the past or best practices from other organizations. The Lean office is truly teaching the organization to problem solve using Lean tools and methods and is hamstrung if no one on the team has these technical skills and experience.

I am not recommending a full team of industrial engineers, but I am recommending one or two seasoned Lean technical team members (they could be engineers, business majors, or clinicians with strong technical Lean experience). Industrial engineers that have specialized in Lean and have a solid track record of Lean projects, coaching, teaching, and facilitation are a great source of talent. You want your senior Lean healthcare coaches to know more about Lean than you do, if possible!

Hiring a solid clinician or two will help connect the Lean office to the floor and help prevent hospital staff and leaders from "pulling the wool over your eyes." The team learns to discover what each team member brings to the table. Just like any great sports team, you want to build your Lean office to specific needs. Partner one Lean engineer with a Lean clinical team member so they can learn from each other and get used to supporting each other. They don't have to work on all of their Lean efforts together, but they should be assigned to a common site and regularly meet to share challenges and learn from each other. The team should work together when dealing with site leadership to ensure they can take advantage of their combined talents.

Some of the best Lean coaches come from the business side of healthcare as well. There may be key managers or directors who have a passion and talent for LDM and Lean (as you deploy LDM you will see/find these individuals). These folks aren't going to have the Lean experience or meet other key requirements, however they may be respected leaders within the organization who can help you deploy much more effectively. When promoting such a leader from within, be sure to assess their technical Lean deficiencies and build that into their unique development plan. It may be helpful to have the Lean team help you with that assessment and the development plan. Bringing in too many Lean coaches who have great leadership and respect, but very little actual Lean technical knowledge can eventually lead to "watering down" the Lean methodology. It's key to remember that the Lean office isn't about being the smartest clinician or the best leader; it's about teaching the organization to problem solve using Lean methods.

How Big Should the Lean Office Be?

The size of the Lean office is driven by the "value" they can create. Early on the organization will need enough Lean team members to support LDM implementation and Lean projects that escalate from staff and leaders. The speed of your LDM implementation should not move faster than leadership can support or keep up with.

Typically one senior Lean coach and one junior Lean coach can support LDM implementation and supporting Lean projects for a small to medium size regional medical center or hospital. For larger systems that have multiple hospitals, sticking to the same ratio for medium and smaller hospitals works well. For larger hospitals you may need one senior Lean coach and two junior Lean coaches to support the larger number of Lean projects that will escalate from the LDM boards.

It takes roughly 2–3 years (of consistent, committed effort) for LDM to fully implement across all units, leaders, and staff (sometimes longer if leadership isn't completely on board early on) in a small to medium size hospital. LDM will start generating improvement the first week the boards go up, but for a true LDM culture-shift across the hospital it generally takes around 1.5–2 years (full implementation around 2–3 years). At this point your senior Lean coach can either support another hospital LDM implementation (keeping the original hospital supported with weekly visits to the senior leader LDM board and rounds to ensure LDM doesn't slide back) or focus on higher-level Lean transformation (Hoshin planning or Lean strategy deployment, Lean layout/3P Lean design, etc.).

Lean team members will eventually look to grow within the organization so it's very important for the Lean office leader to actively work with Lean team members on their individual growth plans. Junior Lean coaches will hopefully develop into senior Lean coaches within 2–3 years and senior Lean coaches may look to move into more senior operational roles after 2–3 years or so. This upward movement is a good thing for LDM and Lean in the organization as the Lean office becomes a pipeline for leadership roles. Senior Lean coaches work so closely with senior leadership and staff at their respective sites that growth into the leadership team of that site or even beyond is a natural thing.

Measuring performance for Lean coaches can be a sensitive topic with many Lean office leaders. Lean coaches teach, coach, facilitate/lead projects but have to work through leaders and staff to implement LDM and Lean and ultimately drive improvement on key organizational goals. Early on measuring the ability of the Lean coach to teach and coach LDM to leaders and staff is going to be key. LDM board audits are a good way to measure the effectiveness of a Lean coach. The Lean office leader can audit Lean coaches weekly to ascertain progress and give appropriate coaching and feedback in a timely fashion. LDM board audits can be measured by their maturity level. Boards that have clear symptoms (goals) and are tracked daily with the gaps being addressed in their diagnosis (analysis) section and treatment plan (action plan) is a base level of maturity. LDM boards that have escalated ideas for leadership to resource/support and have more detailed analysis on their gaps may be a higher level of maturity, while boards that have all of these attributes and have treatment plans that show actions implementing and progress toward their symptoms/goals may be yet a higher level of maturity.

Another measurement for Lean coaches is their ability to develop leaders to round effectively.

Leader round audits can be conducted by the Lean office leader as he or she visits each facility. The audit schedule can be displayed in the Lean office for all Lean coaches to see and prepare for (Lean office version of Leader daily discipline). The Lean office leader simply follows an existing leadership round with a Lean coach to observe the effectiveness. Leadership rounds are going to have some variation from leader to leader based on their personality and style, however the round itself should cover the key components of an effective round.

- Is the Leader rounding consistent?
- Is the leader allowing the team to explain their LDM board symptoms, diagnosis, and treatment plan and what ideas they need escalated?
- Is the leader following up on escalated ideas?
- Is the leader celebrating small wins and valiant failures that taught us something?
- The Lean coach doesn't have direct control over all of these criteria, but the criteria do reflect the development of Leader rounds with that particular leader and is an important measure.

Auditing Leader daily discipline schedules will also tell the Lean office leader how well LDM is maturing. Leader daily discipline audits can simply be a review of a leader's schedule to see how often he or she rounds with whom and when he or she gets to escalated ideas and support of Lean projects.

Measuring Lean coaches also means measuring Lean project effectiveness. Lean coaches are often very quick to get pulled into so many Lean projects that they can't keep up with their LDM work, so just make sure the projects your Lean coaches are supporting tie back to the LDM boards. Encourage more smaller projects like A3's or mini-Kaizens versus larger scale VSM projects that take more staff, more time and are much more complex. The volume of Lean projects is less important as the quality and impact of the project. Audit the Lean coaches' documentation for evidence of effective use of Lean tools and methods. Results are important but the effective use of the Lean method is equally important.

Measuring the development of the site leadership team (for senior Lean coaches) is key. Does the site leadership team have an LDM board? Are they managing their LDM board effectively? Are they resourcing/following up with escalated ideas from lower level LDM boards? Are they making progress toward their goals? Are they engaged? Are they supporting Lean Projects? The Lean office leader can simply attend the site senior leader's LDM review to audit the progress.

Lean coaches have a tendency to "go rogue" sometimes as they develop their sites. It's important for the Lean team to stay connected and collaborate on LDM and Lean implementation. The Lean office leader needs to measure how well the Lean coach works with his or her peers and collaborates on projects, teachings, and so on. Is the junior Lean coach getting the support he or she needs from their senior coach to be successful? Is the junior Lean coach actively engaging the senior coach to get the help he or she needs? Do the Lean coaches collaborate on projects that affect other sites and coaches?

Creating a Lean team culture that fosters collaboration will pay huge dividends over the long haul. Lean team members that are comfortable sharing ideas and supporting each other frees up the Lean office leader to spend more time with senior leadership and the Board of Trustees.

Chapter 10

Lean Change Management

Lean Daily Management (LDM) by design will create a new cadence and rhythm for change that starts with new senior leadership behaviors (rounding, LDM board management, Leader daily discipline, etc.) and then quickly introduces new middle management and front-line staff behaviors. LDM change is truly 80% behavioral and 20% head game (developing great plans).

All training and coaching should be done just in time (e.g., train a group of new leaders on how to build their LDM boards, round, and build their leader daily discipline then start rounding and tracking LDM boards the next day!). Leaders and the Lean coach will need to identify which units and middle managers to start LDM with first. Some initial criteria identifying the first leaders are as follows:

- Is the leader looking to learn and grow (develop) within the organization?
- Does the leader have any Lean Six Sigma or process improvement experience?
- Is the leader coachable?
- Is the leader respected within the organization? (by staff and other leaders)?
- Is the leader able to coach and develop others?
- Has the leader been in the organization long enough to understand the culture?

Identifying the "best" first few leaders and front-line units to stand up LDM will have a dramatic impact on your ability to deploy LDM to remaining leaders and front-line units. Pulling these first few "early adopters" in and getting them involved in the LDM deployment road map/plan will give them a sense of ownership for the roll out and will give your Lean office the leverage they will need to deploy much faster with greater adoption of our new LDM behaviors.

Leaders and staff truly learn best from each other. Where possible, start to stand up local LDM "experts" or "embedded coaches" that you can refer other leaders and staff to. These local experts may not have the time or skill to coach other leaders on all the pieces of effective LDM, however they can show novice LDM leaders and staff how their LDM process works and give them a general sense of what is expected. Once novice leaders and staff have had a chance to review and learn a bit from their peers on how LDM works, the learning curve is reduced dramatically and the Lean office can come in and really get to the "nitty-gritty" of building their LDM boards, leadership rounds, and leader daily discipline.

Some of the local LDM "experts" may be able to help their peers build their initial LDM boards, but the Lean office should still go through and ensure all LDM boards have appropriate symptoms, diagnosis, and treatment plans with escalated ideas. The leader rounding process will ensure LDM board are "up to snuff" as well.

The toughest change will come from senior leadership, not the front lines. Front-line staff will generally follow the actions and behaviors of their leaders. Focusing your Lean team on senior leadership first and foremost will be key; don't get ahead of your "headlights." Moving too fast to middle and front-line leaders/staff before the senior leader is "ready" (consistently and effectively rounding and tracking their LDM boards as well as following their leader daily discipline) will create frustration at all levels. Some senior leaders will catch on fast and are natural LDM leaders; other leaders will quickly revert to traditional "firefighting" management styles. Ideally your chief executive officer (CEO) will be your LDM "expert" for the senior leadership team. Getting the CEO to adopt LDM behaviors should be job number one and the Lean coach and Lean sensei should be coaching the CEO daily until leadership rounding, LDM board management, and leader daily discipline are consistent.

If for some reason the CEO isn't able to become your LDM champion for the remaining senior executives, identifying a respected senior leader that LDM comes naturally to will help the Lean office reinforce LDM behaviors with his or her peers. Once senior leadership is actively rounding and managing their LDM boards, it will become a daily habit; that's the power of

LDM (behavioral change must be reinforced daily over time, with some sort of reward for it to become a habit).

The reward for the senior leader is the feedback and engagement they get from their middle managers and staff as they round. Rounding is the most powerful change behavior in LDM. LDM boards give focus and create local problem solving; however without effective leader rounds, those LDM boards will soon lose enthusiasm and start to collect dust. Leadership rounds set the daily expectation for improvement (vs. the typical monthly expectation in most organizations). Rounds also give middle managers and front-line staff ownership and the leader who is rounding is there to learn, understand, and support their ideas, not the other way around necessarily. The leader that is rounding is there to simply make sure that the LDM process is being followed and to help staff on those problems, issues, and actions that they are stuck on.

The reward for front-line staff is daily recognition from their leader for either a job well-done or effective problem solving on those gaps on the LDM board. Before LDM, senior leaders simply blamed poor performance on bad middle managers, lack of training, or other "generalizations" and staff never really felt "connected" to performance. With LDM, staffs are clearly connected to performance. Staff can clearly and easily tell whether they had a great day or a subpar day and what their analysis (diagnosis) and actions (treatment plan) are to move them in the right direction. Once staff and leaders can clearly and easily connect the dots to performance daily, their anxiety starts to go down dramatically.

Quick test: What causes anxiety in your work area and with you specifically? If anxiety is coming from performance-related issues at work, how can LDM help your area?

Reinforcement is another way to keep the LDM changes moving forward. It may be helpful to partner with other hospitals or healthcare organizations that are trying to implement their own LDM system to tour each other's sites. Constructive feedback from outside organizations or your "Lean sensei" from time to time keeps the organization energized about their progress and moving forward on those areas they might be weak on.

As we mentioned previously in this book, creating an annual "LDM fair" for leaders and staff to showcase some of their achievements, struggles, failures, and learnings is a great way to keep LDM alive and well. Recognizing the "most improved" LDM boards, best LDM "story," and those key local LDM experts who have been supporting LDM deployment all year long makes the emotional connection to LDM possible. At some point the organization may want to simply rename LDM their company "daily management" system.

Working closely with your human resources leaders to build LDM into new employee orientation, and the organizational training program will enable the Lean office to reach more staff and keep LDM front and center. As discussed in the LDM and Strategy Deployment chapter (Hoshin), linking LDM goals to staff performance reviews will accelerate LDM adoption.

The HR department will be a key partner with ongoing development of Lean leaders as well. LDM should be built into the existing leadership training and development program. The Lean office can work with HR to codevelop and codeliver LDM training material to leaders and staff. Collaborating with HR gives HR leaders and staff ownership for the training material and allows the Lean office to reach more staff and leaders. HR will help give LDM and Lean the organizational exposure it simply won't get without HR's support.

HR will become one of the Lean office's most valued partners in deployment of LDM and Lean methods. As more LDM boards go up and staff and leaders start to demand more basic Lean training than the Lean office may be able to deliver, HR can step in and support some of the more basic Lean training courses such as A3 problem solving and basic LDM fundamentals. Working closely with the chief HR officer to identify key HR leaders and staff that can support the Lean office with some of these basic Lean training courses will accelerate LDM and Lean deployment. Those HR leaders and staff identified to support Lean should shadow senior Lean coaches to learn basic Lean tools and methods and then learn to teach them. The best way to learn Lean basics is to participate on a Lean fundamentals project such as building an LDM board, learning how to round effectively, A3 problem solving, standard work, or a 5S event.

One of the "Achilles heels" of most Lean offices and Lean transformations is the inability to not only show hard dollar savings early on, but more importantly the inability to develop strong ties with the chief financial officer (CFO). Every Lean office leader's number one job is to get and keep the CEO engaged and supporting Lean transformation; however in parallel the Lean office needs to quickly develop a strong relationship with the CFO and the chief HR officer.

As mentioned earlier, HR is key to Lean training, tying LDM board goals to the performance review system, and Lean leader development. The CFO is key to establishing and maintaining the "value" of the Lean office and Lean transformation. All Lean transformations have their ups and downs (kind of a life cycle). Early on most Lean implementations get a lot of energy and support; however at some point every Lean transformation hits a plateau. The plateau could come from new leadership with new ideas that challenge Lean principles or they could come from new financial pressures, the list goes on and on.

At some point, any good CFO is going to want to understand the "value" of the Lean office. If your Lean office hasn't already developed a strong relationship with the CFO and very clear guidelines for what constitutes hard dollar and soft dollar savings (benefits bank), it will be very hard to convince any CFO of value after the fact. As you work with your CFO on their LDM implementation, it may be helpful to offer Lean office resources to help support some of their key efforts. Revenue cycle improvement is a great place to start. An LDM board focused on denials has the potential for real hard dollar savings while at the same time giving the CFO and their team a solid opportunity to see and learn the power of LDM and eventually higher level Lean tools and methods.

Working closely with the CFO to develop a "benefits bank" and supporting process for collecting hard dollar and soft dollar benefits will give the CFO a sense of ownership and start to show the hard dollar value of the Lean office. Historically many Lean practitioners and Lean offices have shied away from focusing on hard dollar saving Lean projects to avoid staff perceiving the Lean office as just a "cost cutting" program. Expense reduction, cost cutting, and revenue enhancement is tied into many Lean projects throughout the organization, but is very rarely captured in a structured way that is aligned with the CFO's definition of value.

It may be helpful for the Lean office to present to the CFO quarterly benefits bank of hard and soft dollar savings and any revenue enhancing projects. Getting the Lean office used to keeping up with hard and soft dollar savings early on will keep them aware of their "value" as well as the impact of their Lean projects to other key organizational measures such as patient satisfaction that may not have a direct link to the general ledger.

Large scale LDM transformations (across multiple hospitals or sites) pose a challenge to the Lean office. Typically it's best to start by focusing your Lean office (who are still learning a bit about LDM themselves) with one site/hospital first. Working closely with one CEO and senior leadership team allows the Lean office to give each senior leader the time they need to truly get off to a great start and develop strong LDM behaviors.

This site will become the "go to" hospital for all future sites to learn from. Many Lean transformations have grand visions of pushing out training and coaching to all hospitals all at once in the hope of each site moving steadily along. The risk with this approach is that some sites will inevitably lose steam and get bogged down or frustrated and the Lean office will lose valuable time trying to fix failing LDM sites instead of spending more energy developing one world class LDM site that others can more easily learn from.

As you develop your model site, quickly incorporate that leadership team and key staff into your LDM training. Try to establish tours of your best and some of your "in progress" LDM boards and let your staff do most of the talking (clinicians tend to learn better from other clinicians). Additionally try to share leadership rounds and leader daily discipline from your model site in your training as well. This site will go a long way to establishing how the rest of the organization will deploy LDM and Lean and their examples will give the rest of the organization an example of what LDM looks like within the organization (vs. examples in training that may come from outside the organization).

Developing your own LDM training workshop (vs. a lecture type course) will give staff and leaders the "know how" to build their LDM boards, leader daily discipline and leader rounds; however staff and leaders learn more from real examples of LDM in a hospital setting. It may be helpful to look outside the organization initially for an LDM workshop to train your initial site leadership team. Work with your Lean sensei to identify the right LDM workshop as well as site tours of other successful LDM implementations.

Develop your initial site CEO to lead new senior leaders through the leadership round portion of the training. If possible have the CEO do this "real-time" by actually conducting leadership rounds with new leaders in training. After the leadership round, have the CEO do a little Q&A on the round and have him or her explain what it's meant for his or her site in terms of their goals as well as engagement of staff.

Engaging the best LDM boards and leaders at your model site in training has a side benefit of developing them further on LDM. As any teacher will tell you, when you teach a topic, it forces you to learn that topic deeper and learn about it in a way that practicing alone doesn't quite do. Engaging site leaders to teach also brings out pride in their site and the progress they have made. The teaching site becomes an extension of the Lean office over time, where additional Lean methods and tools can be developed and implemented and then deployed to the rest of the organization.

Many Lean offices will develop their own Lean websites on the company intranet to push out Lean tools and templates and share Lean successes in the hope that staff and leaders will take valuable time out of their day to visit their site. It may be more effective to work with the communications team or even the marketing team to create a better communication channel that staff and leaders will plug into to get Lean info and support. Pushing too much information out too early takes valuable time away from the Lean office to do more meaningful LDM work on the hospital floor before the organization is really ready to listen. Working with the communications department ensures that the Lean message and information are aligned with other organizational initiatives. Key messages and training events can be developed and communicated (change management plan) with the communication department and senior leaders to ensure your LDM messages come from the right leaders at the right time with the right message.

LDM and Lean can create a lot of anxiety and questions from staff and leaders. Lean and process improvement generally makes most staff and leaders a little fearful because the initial assumption is that staff-cuts are soon to follow. The Lean message must be closely aligned with meeting the organization's goals and not just about cost cutting. Lean is designed to bring out the best ideas from front-line staff to achieve organizational goals, which means first and foremost creating a safe environment for those ideas to surface. Communicating regularly how Lean helps clinicians deliver higher quality and safer care to their patients is a great place to start with your Lean change management plan.

Most staff will not have the time and inclination to read Lean "propaganda" written on the organizational website. Most of the time, the best Lean communication comes from the chain of command. Most staff are so busy that they don't really stop and listen to many new organizational efforts unless their immediate supervisor shares it with them personally and takes the time to answer questions. Developing a front-line supervisor LDM and Lean frequently asked questions sheet gives front-line leaders a tool to start having meaningful conversations with their staff about LDM and Lean.

As mentioned earlier in this book, developing and refining the model site's leader daily discipline to include when and how often leadership rounds with staff LDM boards, how escalated ideas are managed and resourced, and when senior leadership reviews their key organizational goals at their LDM board will become the template for LDM at other sites. It may be helpful to set up a review of the model site's leader daily discipline with other site leadership teams to get them started on their LDM deployment. Site leaders learn best from other site leaders, so the more you can engage your model site's leadership team the better.

Creating a little friendly competition across sites is a great way to accelerate the adoption of LDM and Lean principles. Creating an LDM assessment (LDM assessment conducted by the Lean office) and tracking/posting the scores for each site on the senior leadership LDM board month to month is a great way to track progress and drive friendly competition among sites. Something as simple as listing a percentage of LDM boards in place and being rounded on per site per month can keep LDM deployment in front of senior leaders.

LDM assessments can be conducted by the Lean office or by the HR department or on an honor system from the site itself. LDM assessments are meant to ensure that the key components of LDM are in place (leadership rounds, leader daily discipline and LDM boards). Each component of the LDM system is graded based on adoption and effective use. The assessment is meant to give the site an overall LDM adoption score, but also to give the site greater insight into where there may be gaps in their LDM system that need attention.

Physician Buy-in to LDM and Lean

Physicians tend to be the last to adopt LDM and Lean principles for several reasons.

Physicians typically need "data" from respected sources that LDM and Lean will help their practice and patients. Physicians are trained in evidence-based medicine and expect solid evidence that LDM and Lean work.

Putting together a physician white paper (I recommend the Institute for Healthcare Improvement's "Going Lean in Health Care" white paper) to share with physicians gives them some good data and facts from respected healthcare organizations that have already implemented Lean with great effect. Highlighting key pieces of the white paper gives the busy physician a chance to get right to the core of why LDM and Lean are so key to improving their practice.

"Time Crunch"

Most physicians are already so busy with their patient demands, administrative work, and associated meetings that the prospect of learning and piloting something "new" means something else on their schedule must be set aside, or it could mean a longer day with less time for family. Each physician needs to know how much time LDM and Lean will take out of their day. Additionally, helping physicians understand how LDM and Lean start to eliminate wasteful time killers and ultimately give them more time for their patients will be key.

Physicians tend to learn best from other physicians that have lived in their high stress, highly regulated world. Within every hospital or clinic there will be 5%–10% of the physician team that are very progressive and are already experimenting with Lean or other improvement methods. Work with the most respected of these physicians to incorporate LDM and Lean first and then help "sell" LDM and Lean to their fellow physicians.

Patient Safety First

Lean is often perceived by physicians as doing more with less, which sounds great to management but not so great to physicians. In the physician's mind Lean will push more and more work down to the physician and his or her staff. Creating a physician-centric LDM and Lean workshop or short course gives physicians a chance to learn Lean among peers and understand that Lean is about eliminating waste, not staff.

Physicians are trained to be problem solvers and not necessarily coaches per se, so the Lean philosophy of the best ideas to improve the practice coming from the front line (their medical assistants [MAs], licensed vocational nurses [LVNs], registered nurses [RNs], and themselves) may not resonate initially. Coaching physicians that improvement is 20% head knowledge and 80% behavior (measuring and tracking goals daily, understanding gaps in performance, and looking for root causes to those gaps and developing ideas to address those root causes, LDM cycle) makes it easier for them to be open to staff's ideas.

Tracking physician performance on LDM boards is not something that many physicians will readily embrace as well. Each physician has what he or she believes to be unique differences in their practice that may not lend themselves to traditional measurement. The idea of visually tracking and measuring the performance of their practice for all to see can create anxiety with many physicians. Achieving buy-in of physicians with LDM involves first engaging their medical directors and the chief medical officer (CMO) in LDM. Many medical directors carry a partial panel of patients along with their responsibilities of being a medical director, which makes it a bit harder to get time on their schedule for LDM development. Working with the medical directors to identify key goals that each physician may pick from to start with their LDM board gives the provider some power over what they track and measure and ensures alignment with organizational goals.

LDM boards in the hospital tend to focus on measures that front-line staff deal with to engage them in problem solving and oftentimes the physician may or may not be engaged or involved in their unit's LDM board. As you work with your CMO and your medical directors to engage key physicians in LDM early on, try to identify specific measures that your initial key physicians have control over and that aligns with the medical director's goals. Once identified, get these physician-centric goals up on the unit LDM board (don't build another LDM board just for the physicians, try to bring the unit together on one unit LDM board).

In the previous chapters we discussed how unit managers and directors rounded with their unit LDM boards and front-line staff. With our physicians, the leadership rounds need to be led by their respective medical director (unit manager or director can come along, but the medical director is leading the round). Once medical directors are consistently rounding with their physicians on their key LDM board goals and measures, physician ideas will start to escalate and the medical director will need help resourcing and implementing some of these ideas. Try to incorporate escalated ideas/actions from medical director rounds with the existing medical director leadership meetings with the CMO.

Because there are so many unique specialties and practices within the hospital, it may be helpful to develop a high level LDM board for the CMO and his or her medical director's leadership meeting. Each medical director can present progress on their key physician LDM boards. As actions/ideas are escalated from each medical director and their LDM boards, the medical directors and CMO can prioritize and resource those actions accordingly. The Lean office becomes a valued resource that is now actively supporting the CMO and his or her medical directors with their toughest action items and as trust is gained, LDM can be deployed across more and more physicians. Tying these key physician LDM board goals to compensation will accelerate the adoption of LDM boards by physicians.

Keeping physicians engaged is an ongoing process. New medical directors and CMOs will need to learn LDM and practice it. New physicians will need to learn about LDM as part of their orientation (either HR or the Lean office can support the orientation of new physicians with an introduction to LDM piece within the overall orientation for physicians).

Nurses make up the greatest number of staff in the hospital by far and are absolutely vital to any Lean transformation. Building a strong relationship with your chief nursing officer (CNO) will be essential to gaining nursing engagement and involvement. Much like the physicians, tailoring LDM workshops for charge nurses and nurse directors allows nurses to learn alongside other nurses on measures and goals relevant to their world. Work with your CNO and senior nursing leaders to identify LDM board goals for front-line nursing LDM boards. Many nursing floors will already have quality measures that are being tracked in some form or fashion, but don't have the complete LDM system in place (symptom, diagnosis, and action plan). Nursing is usually one of the first groups that grabs hold of LDM, because they are already used to tracking key quality measures such as fall rates of patients, infection rates, hand washing, and so on by floor or unit, so adding the additional structure of the LDM board and the supporting leadership rounds is just a natural next step.

Using LDM on a quality metric that the unit nurses are struggling with is often a great way to gain buy-in to the process. Central line–associated blood stream infections (CLABSI) are often tough to keep within target or goal due to the large number variables that play into these infections. Using LDM on CLABSI is a great place to start with those floors or units that struggle with it.

Working closely with quality metrics means building alignment with your quality director or manager. Many quality managers have an understanding of Lean Six Sigma, but may feel that it's more of productivity, cost cutting, expense reduction methodology and may or may not want to "play" with the Lean office initially. The quality manager's primary concern first and foremost is quality so anything that takes staff's time away from quality can raise concerns. LDM may appear to do that initially as new boards come up with new measures that each particular unit needs to focus on.

The quality manager has been driving quality for quite some time within the organization (well before any Lean implementation), so any successful LDM implementation must respect that fact. As you work with nursing and their floor/unit LDM board goals, be sure to keep the quality manager engaged first. Build a partnership with the quality manager to help them in their job to keep organizational quality at its highest. Reassure the quality manager that LDM is there to support them, not the other way around. Conduct quality rounds with the quality manager so they can see firsthand the power of LDM and help them with escalated quality actions/ideas.

Building alignment with your quality manager will prevent competition for resources, redundant, overlapping work for the floor staff and essentially create a bigger "improvement" team. The quality director continues to use traditional quality tools (which by the way are all Lean Six Sigma tools as well) and add LDM and Lean tools to their toolbox as well. And both the Lean office and the quality team work together to tackle the toughest quality issues.

Chapter 11

Deploying LDM in Your Organization

Step 1:   *Identify your Lean sensei*

Finding an external Lean sensei to help identify and develop your Lean team and gain senior leadership buy-in is one of the key differences between Lean transformations that flounder and those that get traction fast. The Lean sensei's scope of work should be defined really well so everyone is clear on when the Lean sensei should depart.

Step 2:   *Build your Lean team*

Hiring key senior and junior Lean coaches to support key senior leaders and sites is the most important decision the Lean office leader will make. Getting the team focused on Lean daily management (LDM) and small supporting Lean projects will keep everyone on the same page, saving more advanced Lean principles for later.

Step 3:   *Identify or develop an LDM workshop or training course*

Your Lean sensei can help identify or develop a solid LDM workshop that can become the foundational course for teaching senior leadership and middle management.

Step 4:   *Senior leadership LDM workshop*

A key step in any LDM deployment is training and education of senior leadership. Senior leadership needs to understand and practice LDM first and foremost. A quick two-day workshop usually gives senior leadership the principles and understanding of how LDM works and what it means for them as leaders. Immediately after or during the workshop, the senior leadership team needs to develop their LDM board with key organizational metrics and goals (see example) and start huddling with a seasoned Lean coach.

Lay out initial leader daily discipline during the workshop for your senior leader—LDM board development (which goals will you review on which days of the week and when and how will the team conduct leader grand rounds).

LDM boards are the first natural piece of LDM to deploy, so take baby steps with the senior leaders and learn and practice effective LDM board management first.

Step 5:   *Establishing senior leadership cadence with LDM boards (improvement cadence)*

Senior leadership often will be the most challenging but most important level of the organization to develop—don't go it alone—pull in all the help you can to develop your senior leaders. Senior leaders already have more work than they can fit into their schedule and will struggle to find time to fit in daily huddling and leader rounds no matter how good their intentions are. Integrating some of each senior leader's key projects and issues into the daily LDM problem-solving session can win over most of your senior leaders to commit to the LDM board reviews and rounds. Remember they need to feel like LDM will make their workload easier not harder!

As you stand up your senior leadership LDM board, work with each senior leader to own at least one key metric on the board (specifically one that relates to their departmental goals). Work with each senior leader to gradually take over LDM board review (symptoms, diagnosis, and treatment plan with escalated ideas) for their particular metric. I like to set the expectation that after 3 weeks (essentially three facilitations on their metric) each senior leader takes over facilitation of their metric and goal.

Some senior leaders may not feel completely comfortable facilitating in front of their peers, so it's OK to allow that leader to bring in a staff member to help them as needed; however keep ownership of that metric and goal with the senior leader.

Pick a day for each key organizational goal (i.e., Tuesday—growth, Wednesday—patient satisfaction, Thursday—quality, Friday—productivity, etc.) Try to keep the initial senior LDM board to four or five goals to start and over time you can add additional goals to a particular day and either cover two goals in one day or alternate goals week to week.

Senior leadership LDM boards are often bigger (wider) than your middle management and front-line boards. They will have four to five key organizational measures and goals with greater detail on the diagnosis and treatment plan sections than a middle management or front-line board. Pick a room that's big enough to support the board as well as 8–12 senior leaders standing (chairs are not necessary as LDM problem-solving sessions are conducted standing up). If there's not an available room, look for a section of wall that doesn't have high traffic. Have your CEO's executive assistant set up the daily LDM board reviews to ensure it's on all your senior leaders' calendars including the CEO.

Step 6: *Document your senior leader daily disciplines*

Make sure to include what days senior leadership will review LDM boards and when they will round. Make sure leader daily disciplines are in their calendar as recurring events. Include coaching and development time for each senior leader (maybe 15–20 minutes before their leader rounds) to ensure each senior leader is getting the personal time needed to develop their LDM skills and those of their staff.

Step 7: *Deploy key middle management and front-line LDM boards*

As senior leadership begins managing their LDM board daily and developing a rhythm or cadence, start working with each senior leader to identify one key middle manager and one key front-line unit to stand up your first front-line LDM boards. As an alternative, work with senior leadership to identify one key service line (to include those middle managers and front-line units) to develop your initial LDM boards. Develop a fluid rhythm and consistent cadence for LDM with this manager and front-line unit and their LDM boards. Give yourself enough time for that manager and front-line unit to have comfort with the LDM process (tracking LDM symptoms/goals daily, identifying the gaps in actual vs. expected performance daily in their diagnosis section and finally developing and implementing ideas to address the gaps). Ideas that are not getting traction or need leadership support should be escalating to the director/middle manager board and either getting resolution or making their way up to your senior leader LDM board for resourcing. A good team and manager should take roughly 3–4 weeks to get the LDM system down. Once this manager and team are consistently managing their LDM boards and rounds are in place, our key manager can help us deploy to the remaining units, week by week.

Step 8: *Deploy leader grand rounds*

Pick one day of the week to start leader grand rounds. Either conduct grand rounds by service line or by department, letting your senior LDM board gaps and escalated actions guide you. Coach your senior leadership team through leader grand rounds to ensure that they are effectively pulling in escalated ideas from director level and front-line LDM boards. Coach senior leaders to resource key escalated ideas from director level and front-line LDM boards. Encourage senior leaders to celebrate LDM successes and encourage staff to track and manage their LDM boards daily.

Step 9: *Deploy remaining middle management and front-line LDM boards*

Once we have our key front-line LDM boards and director LDM boards in place, other managers and staff can "see" the process firsthand and begin to build their own LDM boards.

LDM Tip: LDM boards will go through several iterations as leader and team move from lagging output measures to more leading or input measures. The key components of the LDM boards should be maintained, but try to resist the temptation to standardize every little bit of the LDM boards—allow staff and leaders enough room to make the LDM boards their own.

Step 10: *Deploy director/middle management leader rounds*

As soon as leader grand rounds occur, many middle managers will start to "pull" coaching and support for middle management rounds to make sure their LDM boards are ready for senior leadership. Work with those key directors or middle managers to conduct effective daily rounds with their front-line staff on their front-line LDM boards and ensure that escalated ideas/actions are making it to their middle management LDM boards.

Step 11: *Identify key Lean projects from escalated actions/ideas on LDM boards*

Working with middle managers and senior leadership, look for escalated actions/ideas that seem to be systematic and use Lean tools/methods to address them (A3s, Kaizen, or value stream mapping). Create a "pull" for Lean tools and methods. Try to emphasize smaller scope Lean A3 projects that can be quickly implemented/piloted with key front-line units and then deployed rapidly.

Step 12: *Integrate LDM with other enterprise initiatives to align potentially competing resources (this may be the first step depending on how many competing initiatives your organization is dealing with)*

One of the biggest reasons Lean transformations lose steam is failure to integrate with new or existing organizational initiatives. Working closely with clinical quality efforts, new electronic medical record implementations, mergers, new hospital and clinic design and construction, etc. to ensure LDM is continually meeting the needs and demands of the changing organization.

Step 13: *LDM and the "Board"*

Developing an LDM board for the "Board" doesn't necessarily need to wait until Step 10; however as the organization reaches an LDM "tipping point" where more staff and leaders are using LDM than not, it's a good idea to get the "Board" using LDM. Getting the "Board" involved in leadership rounds, LDM board reviews, and leader daily discipline gives them a chance to see the power of LDM firsthand as well as reinforce to all staff and leaders the importance of LDM in the organization.

Step 14: *LDM celebrations and fairs*

As with anything new, the LDM engine will lose steam over time without enough reminders of how big of an impact it's had on staff and our patients. At least once a year take time to celebrate the progress staff has made toward their LDM boards. Make sure to recognize not only the most successful LDM boards and units, but also recognize some of your "most improved" LDM boards as well as some of the "valiant failures" that taught us valuable lessons. Don't underestimate the power of unit-to-unit competition with respect to LDM boards and goals.

Step 15:   *Deploy Hoshin planning*

At this point leadership, middle management, and front-line staff are actively managing their LDM boards and making daily improvements. Deploying Hoshin planning aligns and cascades staff performance goals to organizational strategies and LDM board goals.

Appendix 1: Lean Templates and Forms

1. Symptom Template

Symptom: _____ (Include a goal/target!)

	1	2	3	4	5	6	7	8	9	10	11	12	13	14	15	16	17	18	19	20	21	22	23	24	25	26	27	28	29	30	31

2. Diagnosis Template 1: Graph Paper

Diagnosis: _____

	1	2	3	4	5	6	7	8	9	10	11	12	13	14	15	16	17	18	19	20	21	22	23	24	25	26	27	28	29	30	31

3. Diagnosis Template 2: Fishbone Diagram

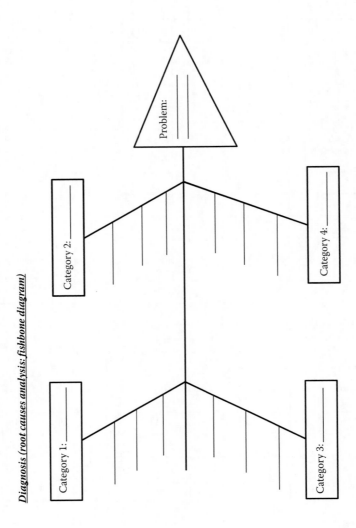

Diagnosis (root causes analysis: fishbone diagram)

4. Diagnosis Template 3: Five Whys

(Diagnosis) 5-Whys

Problem Statement: _____

(State as a problem, not as a solution, a cause, or idea)

Why? _____

    Why? _____

        Why? _____

            Why? _____

                Why? _____

    Why? _____

        Why? _____

            Why? _____

                Why? _____

Why? _____

    Why? _____

        Why? _____

            Why? _____

                Why? _____

    Why? _____

        Why? _____

            Why? _____

                Why? _____

Why? _____

    Why? _____

        Why? _____

            Why? _____

                Why? _____

    Why? _____

        Why? _____

            Why? _____

                Why? _____

5. Treatment Plan Template

Treatment plan:

What:	Who:	When:

6. Leader Daily Discipline Template

Leader daily discipline:

Daily Tasks		
Weekly Tasks		
Monthly Tasks		

7. LDM Board: Three Layers Template 1

> ### *Symptom*
>
> ### *Diagnosis*
>
> ### *Treatment plan*

8. LDM Board: Three Layers Template 2

> ### *Escalation items*
>
> ### *Frustrations and Timewasters*
>
> ### *Wins*

9. Lean Daily Management Checklist

Lean daily management checklist ☑ ☒:

Date/Time: _____   Dept/Area: _____

Leader: _____   Team: _____

(1) Follow up from last huddle:

☐ What did we try? Did it have impact? Are there any next steps?

_____

_____

(2) Today's huddle:

What problem are we focusing on today?_____

Is this a problem that is worth solving and that we can realistically improve?_____

If not, what is a more meaningful metric that we can "move the line"?_____

Do we know what is really causing the problem?_____

Do we have any ideas that we can try between this week and next week
to improve?_____

Have we updated the board to reflect today's discussion?_____

What do we need to do to prepare for a meaningful discussion tomorrow/next
week? _____

(3) Reflection:

How long did the huddle take (15 minutes or less)?_____

What went well?_____

What didn't go well with the huddle?_____

10. Prioritization Framework Template

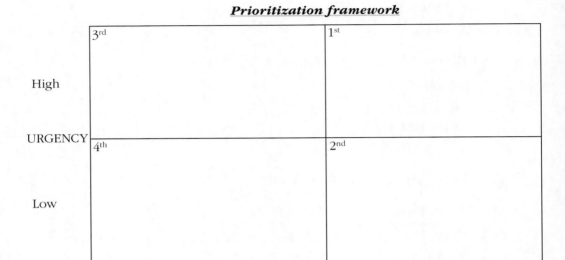

Index